Going
SOLO

**How to survive and thrive
as a freelance writer**

How to Write an Online Course:
From concept to completion one step at a time (eBook)

How to Write a Nonfiction Book:
From planning to promotion in 6 simple steps (7th edition)

Words To Live By:
Reflections on the writing life from a 40-year veteran

The Savvy Ghostwriter: Secrets of an invisible author (eBook)

The Secretary's Secret Weapon:
Arm Yourself With 7 Essential Communication Skills

(Revised and republished as) *Shoptalk: 6 ways to get your*
message across at work (now an eBook)

Secretária Eficiente: Prepare-se para o successo Desenvolva
as sete habilidades essenciais de communicação

Dealing with Difficult People
(Published in the U.S. as) *Solving People Problems*

Polish Your People Skills

Get Organized (co-authored with René Richards)

Planning and Running Effective Meetings
(A self-study course)

How to Write an Effective Resume

Polish Your Professional Image

How to Run a Meeting

Let's Talk:
People With Developmental Disabilities Speak Out

Change is Good! Stories of Community Inclusion

Going SOLO

How to survive and thrive as a freelance writer

BOBBI LINKEMER

LinkUp Publishing

Going Solo
How to survive and thrive as a freelance writer, 2nd Edition
by Bobbi Linkemer

ISBN: 978-0-9885780-5-0

Cover and interior by Nehmen-Kodner: n-kcreative.com
Printed in the United States of America

Published by

LinkUp Publishing

WriteANonfictionBook.com
bobbi@writeanonfictionbook.com
PO Box 440023 • St. Louis, MO 64144

Dedicated to

All of the writers who have allowed me
to be a part of their lives

and to author, Hugh Prather,
who wrote these words:

"If the desire to write is not accompanied by
actual writing, then the desire is not to write."

—from *Notes to Myself*
Real People Press, 1970

CONTENTS

Section II

**Finding Focus: How to Carve Out
Your Niche as a Freelance Writer** **75**

ON MY OWN

free·lance (frê´làns˝) *noun* also free lance
1. A person, especially a writer or an artist, who sells his or her services to employers without a long-term commitment to any one of them.
2. An uncommitted independent.

In one way or another, I have been a freelance writer for almost fifty years. These days, I do it full time. In the beginning, writing was somewhat of a fantasy for me—an impossible, unattainable dream. I played at it for a year or so before I earned my first byline. Only then did I dare to believe that this was something I could do.

I didn't major in journalism or English in college. In fact, my sudden decision to "become a writer" was inexplicable, out of the blue, and out of context. I remember the exact moment when I knew, without doubt, that this was what I was going to do. The problem was that I had no idea how to do it; consequently, I did everything wrong. I read dozens of books on how to write and where to send it once it was

< XI >

written. I tackled just about every subject under the sun, most of which I knew nothing about. I took a night-school course. I wrote poetry, essays, and short stories. I even started a novel. Eventually, I wallpapered an entire wall of my laundry room with rejection slips.

Yet, despite this complete lack of success, I was undeterred. The newspaper reporter who taught the only writing course I ever took had sent me on my way with these life-altering words: "Listen to me," she said, gripping my shoulders (no kidding). "I know talent when I see it, and I see it in you. Keep writing!" I believed her. I kept writing. And when I was just about out of wall space in my laundry room, an editor actually accepted one of my efforts. My first published story was a humor piece called "HBAA: Handball Above All," and it appeared in a national sports magazine.

It took another four-and-a-half years to fill a single portfolio with published clips, few of which earned more than $50. When I finally landed my first "real writing job," it was even more of a fluke than having my first article published in a national magazine. In the space of forty-eight hours I went from the total obscurity of a barely published freelance writer to the high visibility of an editor of a metropolitan magazine. It was called *The St. Louisan.*

Once again, I was in over my head, and thus began the first of many years of on-the-job training—a tough but indelible way to get an education. Every lesson was learned the hard way; every experience was a first; every person I met became a teacher. Photographers taught me to read contact sheets and see the world as they did, through a viewfinder.

< xii >

Writers taught me to discern good writing from bad, fix the bad, or guide the writer through the revision process. Our art director taught me about layout and balance and the "look of the book." Printing and paper salesmen taught me the technical side of creativity, and our one-woman advertising department taught me what it takes to keep a monthly magazine afloat. Finally, the publisher taught me about the privilege of rank, personal agendas, and the meaning of those brackets at the bottom of a profit and loss statement. I didn't even know what a P&L statement was, which turned out to be a very serious flaw.

Perhaps the most important lessons I learned came from freelancers. Since it quickly became apparent that I could not personally write an entire magazine every month, I had to depend on freelance writers, illustrators, and photographers to provide most of the content and color. There weren't a lot of places freelancers could sell their work in those days; if they found one, often they had to deal with an editor who was an egomaniac.

I didn't know enough to have an ego; the word spread that I would see anyone, read anything, look at any portfolio. I met a lot of freelancers that way. It has been forty years since I left that job, and yet my memories are still vivid. We were all very young and eager. We were all at the beginning of our careers. We were all hungry to see how good we really were.

I still have copies of every issue of *The St. Louisan* I helped to create. I treasure them because they were such labors of love for all of us. The writing was fresh and often passionate. The photography and art foretold of brilliant

< xiii >

careers to come. And many of the relationships I formed then still exist today.

Between *The St. Louisan* and my return to full-time freelancing was a steady progression of career moves that took me from magazines to corporations to a quirky little company where I was able to fill in many of the remaining gaps in my professional education. Those were the building years. I honed my skills, broadened my repertoire, enlarged my network, and, at long last, increased my income.

During all the years I worked as a full-time writer, freelancing was something I squeezed in between earning a living, raising my children, and trying to build a life. I did it for many reasons: for money, for the creative outlet, and sometimes just for fun. I never tired of writing, and I never wanted to do anything else for a living; but, increasingly, I found the circumstances in which I was doing it to be unfulfilling at best and stifling at worst. Finally, armed with the smallest of nest eggs, I traded the corporate world for the scary, high-wire act of full-time freelancing. The only safety net I had was that tiny bit of savings. I knew that when it was gone I would be up there on my own. It was a leap of faith, but I took it.

Frankly, I had no idea if anyone would remember me, if businesses hired freelancers, or if one could make a living doing this. Like Alan Alda in *Same Time Next Year,* "I guess I didn't think it through." I must have had a guardian angel or was just plain lucky because the answer to all three questions was *yes.* My long-ago visibility had not completely faded; people knew who I was and took my calls. There was,

< xiv >

at that time, an abundance of work "out there." In fact, it seemed that every major corporation in St. Louis was using freelancers, no matter how large their marketing, communications, or public affairs departments might be.

My little business took off like a rocket, which was a good news-bad news story. The good news was that getting off to a great start built my confidence and reaffirmed my decision to take the leap. The bad news was, when the hard times hit, as they were bound to, I was caught off guard and had no back-up plan.

Somehow, I survived the first business slump. In fact, I have survived more than a few over the years—not always with style or new-found business acumen, often by mortgaging my future to finance my present, and occasionally by asking myself if it was time to get a "real job." I haven't succumbed so far because I came to my senses, business picked up, or no one was breaking down my door to offer me a six-figure salary.

Of course, having finally left the confinement of corporate life and tasted "freedom" for the first time, it would be next to impossible to return to captivity. That's the most compelling reason I am still here and will probably remain here until they cart me off to my final resting place.

"Here" is a tiny enterprise called Bobbi Linkemer & Co., a one-person business operating out of a one-person condo. Who is "and company"? The answer is that, when a project requires additional research, design, illustration, production, printing, or any other specialized service, I call upon experts in those areas to become part of my team. In a business

< xv >

environment where more and more talented people are going out on our own, we become each other's extended companies. That makes it possible for each of us to do what we do best and yet provide our clients with a full array of talent and services, affordable fees, and convenient, on-call "professional partners"—when needed.

I am, in many ways, living in the best of all possible worlds: doing what I love, enjoying the freedom of free-lancing, growing creatively and professionally, and seeking new and bigger challenges. I've often heard it said that every writer has one book inside him or her that wants to come out. This is definitely that book.

< xvi >

INTRODUCTION

Before you read any further, you should know two things: First, though the term "freelancing" can be applied to any number of disciplines, this is a book about freelance writing. It is intended for anyone who wants to be, or already is, writing for a living, in or outside of the safe haven of "a real job." Second, it is not your typical how-to book, even though an abundance of very practical suggestions can be found within its pages.

I know there are *many* other books on this subject in the career sections of any bookstore. Frankly, I was surprised at just how many. Apparently, "going solo" is a hot topic, as more and more writers find themselves striking out on their own for an array of compelling reasons.

Some have no choice: They have been downsized, laid off, reorganized, or even fired, a word that has been replaced

< 1 >

by so many euphemisms that it has all but been obliterated from the language. Others are "following their bliss," either by taking the plunge with little forethought and less money or by having stashed away just enough to take a calculated risk for as long as their savings hold out. A few "just do it." After all, why not? What do they have to lose? If it doesn't work, they can "just do" something else.

Some brave souls dive in with no other source of income, no prospects on the horizon, and only idealism to keep them afloat. Those who are less gutsy, or perhaps more pragmatic, keep their jobs and cautiously stick a toe in the water, writing on the side to see how it feels and if it might some day actually pay the rent. A limited number think it through, plan, and get all their ducks in a row *before* they launch. But, by far, the vast majority of would-be freelancers leaps first and contemplates later, often while still in mid-air.

If any of these descriptions fits you, you're in the right place. If none of them does, but you are or want to be a free-lance writer, you are still in the right place. I have been a freelancer on and off for forty-five years and working at it full time for the last twenty-five. During all of those years, I have been learning my trade by the seat of my pants, so to speak. If they offered degrees or even courses for independent writers, I was unaware of them. In fact, I didn't realize until recently that there were books on every aspect of how to go out on your own without starving to death.

Since it is never too late to learn, I decided to check out a few of these books. While most of them were informative and well written, as I read, I had the feeling that something

< 2 >

was missing. They certainly covered the business of free-lancing in depth and detail—how to start a business, how to land big money assignments, how to tackle any conceivable message or media, how to establish your fees, and much more. These are all very important subjects for a writer to know, and I must admit I learned some new things or was reminded of others I had once known and forgotten. The authors, for the most part, are people who actually have been or are now freelancers. Still, there was this nagging sense that none of these experts had painted the complete picture.

These omissions, I finally decided, were the things I would say to aspiring or working freelancers—what I *do* say when I'm giving a talk or being a mentor or teaching a class. They encompass the personal, the experiential, the intangible lessons I have learned—often the hard way—over the years. These are the kind of insights one rarely encounters in a how-to book; at least, I haven't. Yet, to me, they are the real essence of the freelance life.

Writers are always advised to write about what we know. If there is one thing I know, it is the peaks and perils of the writer's life, particularly the independent, freelance writer's life. I wanted to share that experience and savvy with readers. But I also know there are many other perspectives on freelancing besides mine. I know writers and artists who freelance part time, sometimes, or full time. I know some who tried it, loved it, but for their own reasons, left it and never looked back. I know others who dream of the free-lance life but for lack of money or courage or opportunity,

< 3 >

never took the leap and always wonder if they could have made it on their own.

There are so many other elements of the freelance life that deserve discussion—such traits as talent, curiosity, discipline, and obsession ... the obstacle course of tough choices, tough editors, tough assignments ... the agony of clients who pick your work to pieces, pay late, don't pay at all, or drop you flat without explanation ... and the ecstasy of doing what you love, loving what you do, and being your own boss. Why not write about those things? To me, they are every bit as important as how to set up a home office or an accounting system and the secrets of earning big fees by specializing in annual reports.

Section I, Getting Started: What It Takes to Make It as a Freelance Writer, explores the strengths, skills, and characteristics that are necessary for success.

Section II, Finding Focus: How to Carve Out Your Niche as a Freelance Writer, looks at the choice between trying to "do it all" (writing about anything for anyone in any media) and becoming known for a particular area of expertise (subject matter, industry, type of communications, style, or genre).

Section III, Balancing Act: How to Play the Many Roles of a Freelance Writer examines the challenge every entrepreneur faces—how to assign equal time and energy to your business life, your personal life, and your inner life.

Freelance writing is a creative, intensely personal profession. On one hand, it is far too complex to be captured by a simple formula for success; on the other, it does yield its

< 4 >

secrets over time to those who practice it. As an artist, craftsman, and entrepreneur, there is no freelancer who wouldn't benefit from the advice of a seasoned mentor.

There are many ways to read this book: front to back or a piece at a time. Some or all of it may speak to you, depending on your current situation and needs. My advice is to browse; sample; find what you need, when you need it; and keep it on your shelf as what I hope will become a timeless resource. Above all, become an active participant in an ongoing dialogue with kindred spirits on this exciting journey.

< 5 >

GETTING STARTED:

What it takes to make it as a freelance writer

< 7 >

CHAPTER 1

TALENT

talent (tàl´ent) *noun*
1. A marked innate ability, as for artistic accomplishment.
2. Natural endowment or ability of a superior quality.

"You either have it or you've had it," is a line from Rose's final song in the Broadway play *Gypsy*, and that about sums up the word *talent*. You can learn to write; you can develop the necessary skills; you can perfect the formulas and turn out acceptable copy. In fact, you can be a successful writer without necessarily having talent. I know quite a few people who fit that description. But to be *really* good, to stand out from the crowd, to bring that something special to every piece of writing—*that* requires the real thing.

You don't acquire talent; you are born with it ... or, at least, you are born with an inner spark that can be ignited and tended until it becomes talent. Talent stands out. You know it when you see it. It can knock you flat if you see it in someone other than yourself. I experienced both as a freshman art student in college.

Like all of my classmates, I was struggling—trying my best to figure out what was expected of me and how to produce it—when I encountered a more mature, more

< 9 >

confident fellow student. He was going to school on the G.I. Bill and seemed much older than those of us who were standard-issue eighteen-year-olds. It took only a matter of moments to know that he was "drawing circles" around all of us. He wasn't struggling; he was coasting. Everything he drew or painted, even if it was a collection of pipes in the basement of the art school, had a kind of vibrancy to it, as if it were going to pop right off the drawing board.

He was indisputably good—so good that he was able to "proficiency out" of one class after another until he was *teaching* them, instead of taking them. I was awed. We were all awed. Whatever admiration we may have earned as outstanding artists in high school, here, for the first time, we were in the presence of true talent. Most of us paled in comparison. I certainly did. I could not imagine ever producing anything near the caliber of his work, and I was frankly quite intimidated. Before the next semester began, I had changed my major. Perhaps that was a bit drastic; but I was firmly convinced, as I am even now, that whatever it takes to be a great artist, I didn't have it.

On the other hand, as magic as talent is and as fortunate as one is to be blessed with it, it is far from a guarantee of success in writing or in any other creative pursuit. With it, you have an advantage; without it, you may have to expend more effort. While it is a critical piece in a complex puzzle, it is not the only piece. By itself, talent in art or science or virtually any other field of endeavor has its limits. If you fail to nurture it and build on it, you can be sure it will never completely fulfill its promise.

< 10 >

For several years, I taught a class in feature writing for magazines. The students were all adults and as disparate as people could be. At the beginning of each class, I promised these aspiring writers that if they followed all the steps I proposed, at the end of eight weeks, they would be sending their edited manuscripts to editors who had agreed to read them. This was a straightforward guarantee; no strings. Do the work; reap the rewards.

There were a couple of people in each session who were immensely talented. There were others who were rather average writers. What they all discovered was that talent alone was not going to get their articles into envelopes or in front of eager (well, *willing*) editors. What *was* going to make that happen was hard work and following a process, one step at a time. Those who did the work got a reading; a few were even published. What surprised me at first was that it was the "average" writers who went the distance; most of the time, those with recognizable talent stopped well before the end.

As a book-writing teacher many years later, I saw this same pattern play out again and again. Promising authors who were passionate about writing and publishing their books most often succeeded. Some had talent; some did not. (They all had good editors, by the way). Talent helped, but dogged determination made all the difference.

< 11 >

CHAPTER 2

OBSESSION & DISCIPLINE

ob·ses·sion (eb-sèsh´en, òb-) *noun*
1. Compulsive preoccupation with a fixed idea or an unwanted feeling or emotion, often accompanied by symptoms of anxiety.
2. An often unreasonable idea or emotion.

dis·ci·pline (dîs´e-plîn) *noun*
Controlled behavior resulting from disciplinary training; self-control.

If you asked me what single factor kept me in the game all these years, I would say, without hesitation, *obsession*. It certainly wasn't a life-long desire to write, since, during the first half of my life, the idea of writing for a living had not occurred to me. In fact, for much of my career, it wasn't confidence in my ability, because that was in short supply. In the beginning, I would have to say it wasn't skill, because I had no concept of my role in the writing process. For a while, I honestly believed there was some magic in my little Smith-Corona portable typewriter. All I had to do was turn it on, and out came page after page of coherent writing. How that actually occurred remained a mystery to me for a long time.

< 12 >

When people ask me when I knew, *how* I knew, this was what I wanted to do, I compare my experience to that of Michael Corleone in *The Godfather*. He met a girl in Sicily and was "hit by the lightning bolt" that caused him to love this girl instantly and forever. I can think of no better way to describe my crazy love affair with writing other than to say that I, too, was hit by a lightning bolt. From the moment I first sat down to write, I was hooked instantly and forever.

Nothing else in my life has captured and held my attention so strongly and for so long. When I was working at other full-time jobs, chasing after small children and a large dog, and trying to tape together some semblance of a normal life, I managed to write, even if it was at 2:00 in the morning. I wrote through a divorce, twenty versions of the flu, mono, hepatitis, and pneumonia. I wrote through losses and doubts and wrong turns in my life, through lean times and lush times, through every stage of my children's lives from toddlerhood to adulthood, and through more than four decades of my own life. If that isn't obsession, I don't know what is.

The notion that I could be and would be a writer when there was little or no reason to believe it, was surely "a compulsive, often unreasonable idea or emotion," especially in the early years. To cling to that notion for years, to turn down all offers for anything less than a *real* writing job, and to have only one goal—to become a better writer—are all recognizable symptoms of an obsessive condition for which there is only one cure: to write. And so, I'm still at it, both

< 13 >

astonished and grateful at how long this feeling has sustained itself.

Unfortunately, obsession doesn't automatically translate into discipline. In fact, they may even be contradictory at times. When you are obsessed with something, you think about it constantly and would do it all the time if that were possible. Discipline, on the other hand, requires self-control; you either will yourself to engage or to disengage in an activity. For many writers, actually sitting down to write is sheer agony. The joy is in *having written*, and it takes inordinate fortitude to just begin. For others, of whom I am one, *the act of writing* is hypnotic. I am drawn to the computer and go into a trance the minute I sit down. There is nothing harder for me than getting up and walking away.

I make deals with myself every morning: *I will not turn on the computer until I exercise. I won't even walk into my office until I take a shower and get dressed. I will make five marketing calls before I begin writing.* The deals rarely stick. My discipline evaporates, and there I am, still in my workout clothes—or worse yet, my robe—sitting at the computer "for just a moment," I tell myself. And suddenly it is two in the afternoon, and I haven't moved.

Many people insist that discipline precedes obsession. In my experience, the reverse is true. It takes a great deal of self-discipline to break away from the computer do something as simple as leave the house. I have discovered that attaining discipline is a four-step process, which includes:

< 14 >

1. A goal (knowing what you want to achieve)
2. The decision (to go for it)
3. A plan (that is possible)
4. Action (working the plan)

If the goal is to lose weight, the decision is to get serious about a weight-loss program; if the plan is to exercise or stick to a nutritional program, the action would be to join a gym or Weight Watchers, make a regular date with a workout partner, give up sugar, or whatever else works.

If the goal is to write a one thousand-word article, the decision is to get organized and set aside time to write; the plan is to research your topic, read all the relevant information you have gathered, and make the article a priority; the action would be to sit down and write.

The trick, of course, is to *do* it, rather than muse about it. Discipline is tough. That's why it is so important to know not only *what* you want but also *why* you want it. Without step one, there will be no decision, no plan, and no action.

< 15 >

CHAPTER 3

PROFESSIONALISM

pro·fes·sion·al·ism (pre-fèsh´e-ne-lîz-em) *noun*
1. Professional status, methods, character, or standards.
2. The use of professional performers, as in athletics or in the arts.

What does it really mean to be a professional writer? Years ago, I thought it was just a matter of being *paid*—something, anything—for a piece of writing. The first time I received a check for all of $50, I was sure I had made it. But the thrill didn't last long. For one thing, it was ages between checks. For another, after a while, $50 checks didn't seem fair compensation for what I put into article after article. And, finally, it took four-and-a-half years to fill a single portfolio. It was a very slow process and hardly a lucrative one. On the other hand, it was a fitting beginning to my career in many ways. I pursued every opportunity to write. I gave every project my all. I made very little money. And I questioned my sanity on a regular basis.

Much of that is still true, but I have learned that there is so much more to being a true professional than I ever imagined when I was young. It certainly goes far beyond the financial aspect by which I first measured it. Like "class,"

< 16 >

professionalism is difficult to define; yet, we all recognize it when we see it. There are two perspectives on this subject: one is that of your clients or editors; the other is yours. While there are some measures of professionalism most people would agree on, you won't really know how your clients or editors define it unless you ask them. Asking them, by the way, is a very good idea. How will you know what they think, expect, or value unless you do ask? And if you don't know, how will you be able to evaluate how well you measure up to their criteria? From my own perspective, however, I will consider myself a true professional when:

- **I do my best work on every project, every time.** To me, that means I don't get sloppy or cut corners on small jobs. I have a single set of standards that applies to all of my work, not just the high-paying assignments. When I found myself feeling resentful because I was underpaid for going above and beyond, I decided not to accept any projects under a certain minimum dollar amount.

- **I come through.** I keep promises. I do what I say I'll do when I say I'll do it. This applies to even the smallest things. If I tell someone I will look up a phone number and call them, I try very hard to do it and, more than that, to do it in a timely manner. If I don't, I am haunted by *not* doing it, even if it was more an offhand remark than a promise.

- **I treat people with respect and consideration**—all people, no matter what position they may hold or how

< 17 >

"important" they may be. I have seen too many people ingratiate themselves with senior executives only to turn around and bite off some secretary's head. I don't know what bothers me more—the insincerity of the obsequious behavior or the double standard based solely on status.

- **I can be trusted.** I don't carry tales or betray confidences. I don't talk to one client about another. I don't pad my billable hours. I do express my opinions, even when it may not be what the client wants to hear. Surprisingly, clients *expect* me to tell them what I think. In fact, I believe that is one of the reasons they hire me.

- **I look the part.** Perception is reality. I work hard at creating and nurturing the perception of professionalism in my appearance, attire, attitude, and demeanor. *Everything* reflects what I do and how well I do it, from the message on my voice mail to my wardrobe. My theory is that, if I take great care with how I present myself, it is a good indication that I will take great care with anything I write.

Those are tough criteria, I know, and not easily met. Being 100 percent "professional" 100 percent of the time is akin to being perfect—an unattainable state. On the other hand, becoming a consummate professional is a worthy goal for every professional writer. And unlike perfect, it *is* attainable.

< 18 >

CHAPTER 4

CURIOSITY AND IMAGINATION

cu·ri·os·i·ty (kyur̋ê-òs î-tê) *noun*
A desire to know or learn.

i·mag·i·na·tion (î-màj̋e-nâ´shen) *noun*
1. a.) The formation of a mental image of something that is neither perceived as real nor present to the senses. b.) The mental image so formed. c.) The ability or tendency to form such images.
2. The ability to confront and deal with reality by using the creative power of the mind; resourcefulness.
3. Imagination, fancy, fantasy; the power of the mind to form images, especially of what is not present to the senses.

Curiosity and imagination are two sides of the same coin: one is the unquenchable thirst for knowledge; the other is the process by which we create something entirely new out of that knowledge. It has been said that there is no such thing as a new idea, that everything that exists is already known. If that is true, then curiosity impels us to search for what is known, and imagination sees it in a new and unique form.

< 19 >

It's hard to imagine how or why one might choose to be a writer, especially a freelance writer, without this trait. What would be the incentive, if not to absorb information and reconfigure it in a way that others can enjoy and absorb it as well? Without it, this chosen way of life becomes merely a job—a way to earn a living—and for most of us that's not what it's about.

Curiosity

Curiosity cannot be created or taught when it doesn't exist, but it *can* be nurtured even when only a tiny spark of it exists. If you've ever begun a sentence with the words, "I wonder ...." or followed the thread of a thought around in your head to see where it would take you, or become lost in a subject other people consider boring, or found yourself asking a million questions of someone you've just met, you've got the spark. Now, all that's necessary is to let it catch fire. Here are some ways to fan the flames:

- **Don't be satisfied with just enough research or just enough information to complete the assignment.** Keep digging, keep analyzing, keep seeking a deeper understanding of the material. Eventually, you'll run out of time, you'll run out of sources, or your sixth sense will tell you that one more fact will be one fact too many. That's when you know you've done all you can do, and it's time to write.

< 20 >

- **Get involved with your topic.** Care about it, make it personal, invest yourself. Believe it or not, this will not compromise your integrity as a writer; it will enhance it. If you care, the message will ring true, and the words will come alive; if you don't, the reader will sense—often without knowing why—that something is missing.

- **Think of everything you learn as a thread in a tapestry.** If you stick with it long enough, no matter what kind of writing you do, patterns begin to emerge. You'll find that no idea exists in isolation and that every piece of knowledge is inexplicably linked to every other piece. The more you learn, the more obvious those links will become. New ideas combined with long-forgotten snippets of information give birth to deeper insights, which, in turn, become new threads in the pattern.

Imagination

Tapping into the imagination is not something only novelists, poets, and promotional writers do. It is something every good writer does, consciously or instinctively. Imagination is our secret weapon, our special ability to put an original spin on virtually anything, no matter how tired or hackneyed it may seem. A good writer looks at the assignment, the raw data, the blank page and sees something no one else sees—a unique perspective, a hidden pattern, the very heart of the matter. Like combining chemical elements, in go bits and

< 21 >

pieces of information, impressions, and interpretations; out comes something completely new, one of a kind.

If curiosity can be nourished, like a tiny plant, is that also true of imagination? Why do some people view the world through a kaleidoscope of colors and shapes, while others see it in black and white, straight lines that go from here to there? Can imagination be created out of the raw material of our minds, or is it something one has or doesn't have, like blue eyes?

If we are to believe many of the great writers, imagination is part of our human birthright. If the spark exists, the hidden light is just waiting to shine. What turns an analytical thinker into an imaginative one? Try these suggestions.

- Open your mind to other ways of looking at things. If someone else suggests a different perspective, don't dismiss it out of hand. Delve, explore, examine. Turn it over in your mind. Add to it. Add it to the mix of ideas on the table.

- Don't be satisfied with your first take on anything. Don't be in a hurry to get on with it and hit the computer. Unless you're on a killer deadline, step back and give it some air. See what else comes up. Walk around it (figuratively), and chances are you'll see it from a different angle.

- Don't settle for the way you've always done it. If you usually surf the Web or use the business library, find an expert to interview. If you plunge into writing the minute

< 22 >

you finish your research, try giving yourself a day to read and absorb your notes, and sleep on it before you sit down to write. If you polish every sentence as you go, try stream-of-consciousness writing. Just changing your habits will stretch the limits of your imagination.

- Take time to do nothing. Call it meditation, daydreaming, or kickback time. Carve out some time at least once a week for *you*. Go to the park, the zoo, the country. Take a walk, a bike ride, or a drive. Let your mind roam wherever it chooses to go. The idea is to slow down the compulsive thinking/doing mind and give it a break. Just imagine what could come out of such an afternoon!

< 23 >

CHAPTER 5

TRUST IN THE CREATIVE PROCESS

trust (trùst) *noun*
1. Firm reliance on the integrity, ability, or character of a person or thing.
2. Reliance on something in the future; hope.

cre·a·tive (krê-â´tîv) *adjective*
1. The ability to perceive new combinations of information.
2. The ability to imagine and make new or original forms, ideas, or things by transcending traditional thinking.
3. Characterized by originality and expressiveness; imaginative: *creative writing.*

proc·ess (pròs´ès˝, pro´sès˝) *noun*
1. A series of actions, changes, or functions bringing about a result.
2. A series of operations performed in the making or treatment of a product: *a creative process.*

Creativity is a mysterious process. An artist or inventor or scientist takes existing elements — ideas, materials, words — throws them into a pot, stirs them around for a while, and ultimately produces a completely original product. You can

< 24 >

study and analyze these steps up one side and down the other and still never completely grasp how that product is unlike anything that went into that pot or like anything else in the world. It doesn't matter what goes into the mix; what comes out is always unique.

It is a leap of faith to sit down at a computer or drawing board or potter's wheel and know that, somehow, this process will work, even if you have no idea how. The secret of writing and every other form of creativity is to *trust the process*. In this, as in all of life, trust is forged over time.

When I first began to write, the miracle of starting with nothing and ending up with pages of coherent copy was a mystery to me. I knew only that, when I sat down at my little electric portable, something magic happened, but I didn't know where the magic came from. It seemed to have a life of its own over which I had no control. I became fascinated with the process, which never seemed to fail me. Eventually, however, I was able to break it down into five critical steps:

1. **Get the facts.** This is the research phase. Whether you are writing an article, a brochure, a presentation, an annual report, or a book, this is the time to gather information. Your sources can be virtually anything: interviews with experts, the daily paper, scientific journals, the library, or the World Wide Web. You can capture it by taking notes, using a tape recorder, photocopying, or committing it to memory. The important thing is to find out as much as possible about your subject. Even if you

< 25 >

don't have a deadline, you will know intuitively when it is time to stop researching. This is your first test of trust. Before you get to overload, stop.

2. **Feed your subconscious mind.** This is the time to sift through the information you have just accumulated. It is a very important step, but strangely, it is also one many writers do in a cursory manner or ignore completely. Chances are you have a mountain of material; so give yourself plenty of time to read, analyze, organize, and absorb all of it, even if that seems overwhelming. If it takes all day, block out the day, and dive in. The process is a little like cramming for an exam in that you must focus and concentrate. Like the research stage, you will know when you've had enough. Once again, when you feel full to the brim, stop.

3. **Let it percolate.** This is the most difficult step for most writers because it involves consciously, intentionally *not* writing. In fact, do anything *but* write—take a walk, watch TV, make dinner, curl up with a novel, or go to sleep. Don't review your notes. Don't try to organize your thoughts. Don't even think about the project. I have always been a bit fanatic about this step because it is the heart of the creative process. If you posed a problem to your computer, you wouldn't run a race to see who found the answer first; you would let the computer do what it's designed to do. And you wouldn't question how it did it.

< 26 >

Now, let your subconscious do what it was designed to do, which is to process the information you have given it. This is just one more step in trusting the process.

4. **Write.** What separates the pros from the amateurs is knowing *when* to write. This step builds quite naturally on the first three, and, if you've done them in order, you are ready to write. When I plan my time well, I can wait a day between steps 3 and 4. A good night's sleep does wonders for sorting out even the most daunting pile of data. We all approach writing in our own way. Though most of us now use a computer, there are still diehards who pound away on a manual typewriter or fill multiple legal pads with longhand prose. Whatever your style may be, as they say, "If it works, don't break it." This is no time to change.

That rule applies to all of the idiosyncrasies writers develop over time. Are you a stream-of-consciousness writer, who gets it all out as fast as you can and fixes it later; or are you more deliberate—rereading, editing, and perfecting every page or paragraph as you go? Do you do it all in one sitting or break your writing time into chunks? Do you listen to music or insist on total silence? Do you snack all day or forget to eat?

All of these little habits are the frosting on the cake. The cake, of course, is the act of writing, which you may love or hate, do in a timeless trance, or suffer through every agonizing moment. All that matters is that you do it and trust that, when you're finished, what you have

< 27 >

written will be accurate, articulate, and acceptable. How do you know when you're finished? Just like every other step, trust that you will know.

5. **Prune and polish.** Whether you wrote like a person possessed or stopped to manicure every sentence, you will still have to look at your work with a critical eye—to edit, cut, refine—as many times as it takes to meet your own standard of excellence. If you are writing an article, this is the time for spell check, grammar and punctuation rules, stylebooks, and a good thesaurus. If you are writing a book, this is the time for an editor or a copyeditor. Every writer needs an editor. *Every* writer. It is hard to overestimate the importance of this statement. I am a writer and an author; yet, I am always blown away by the mistakes my editors find in my work. I usually have more than one editor; each one catches something the others missed.

That is my "process." Even before I figured out how I was doing what I was doing, I knew it worked. I trusted it completely, and I still do. Let me emphasize that it is neither quick nor easy. Every step takes time, energy, commitment, and discipline. I have never found a shortcut. Writing is hard work—agony for some, ecstasy for others—but rarely effortless. Each of us must find our own process and then learn to trust it.

< 28 >

CHAPTER 6

PEOPLE SKILLS

peo·ple (pê´pel) *noun; plural* people
1. Human beings considered as a group or in indefinite numbers: *People were dancing in the street. I met all sorts of people.*
2. The mass of ordinary persons; the populace.

skill (skîl) *noun*
1. Proficiency, facility, or dexterity that is acquired or developed through training or experience. See synonyms for ability.
2. a. An art, a trade, or a technique, particularly one requiring use of the hands or body. b. A developed talent or ability: *writing skills.*

Writing is often perceived as a solitary process. While there is some truth to that perception, it is only half the picture. I think many people actually visualize writers as holed up in our little garrets, shut off from the world, waiting patiently for inspiration to strike. Needless to say, that is a fairy tale, although—as a writer who spends a great deal of time in one room, on one chair, doing one thing—on some days, I do feel a bit shut off from the world. On the other hand, I wouldn't call my thoroughly modern, fully equipped

< 29 >

little office a garret. Neither do I wait for inspiration to strike; I create my own, on demand, every day.

If I do indeed spend large chunks of time working alone, why are *people skills* on the list of "what it takes"? The answer is that, for the kind of writing most freelance writers do, much of our time is spent switching back and forth between being alone and being with others, which require two entirely different sets of skills. When we are with others, people skills are essential to establishing a genuine connection, to assessing who and what we are dealing with, and to responding appropriately.

Obviously, that is not always easy. If it were, there would be fewer crossed signals and misunderstandings, more satisfied clients and editors, and far less stress involved in freelancing. There would also be little need for all the books and seminars on every conceivable aspect of getting along with others. We take those courses, and we read those books (in fact, I *write* those books) in hopes of finding some magic formula for connecting with people in a meaningful and mutually beneficial way.

While I don't believe there is such a formula, there are some very common-sense guidelines that have stood the test of time. If they have a familiar ring, that's not surprising. In one form or another, we have grown up hearing most of them.

- **Don't treat others as you do not wish to be treated.** This is the universal commandment and the only one any of us will ever need. It applies to anyone in any situation,

< 30 >

any time, anywhere. That certainly includes the world of business. If you don't want to be demeaned, yelled at, harshly criticized, humiliated, ignored, or insulted, it's safe to assume no one else does either. If you appreciate a simple *thank you* or *job well done* for your efforts, you are probably not alone. This is the foundation of people skills.

- **Between stimulus and response you have a choice.** Much of people's behavior is an unconscious, knee-jerk reaction to something someone said or did or some outside event. A situation occurs, and we react, often automatically. A client criticizes your work; a supplier holds up a project; an editor returns your manuscript with an impersonal form letter. What do you do? Chances are, if you are like I am, you get upset. You are instantly hurt or frustrated or disappointed. But what if you paused for just a second and decided *how* to respond, rather than just letting impulse guide you? You might be surprised to see the result. For one thing, you would take control of your own behavior and perhaps even of the situation. No matter how bad something appears to be, a negative reaction on your part isn't going to make it any better. So take a breath, assume you don't know the whole story, and *then* respond.

- **Build every encounter on a foundation of respect.** That includes respect for yourself and respect for the other person. When you have self-respect, you have the courage to be yourself. You never allow yourself to be put

< 31 >

down or poorly treated, and your actions are consistent with your personal values. When you respect others, you remember that they share all of your human qualities; you take the time to hear them out; and you try to understand their point of view, even when you don't agree.

- **Never judge a person until you have walked a mile in his or her shoes.** We make judgments all the time— about people, about appearances, about behavior, about our own and others' work. First impressions are lasting impressions, they say; but they are often totally inaccurate, as well. I come in contact with many people in my work, and, unfortunately, I am not immune to being judgmental. A secretary is uncooperative or rude to me, perhaps more than once, and I form a negative opinion. An editor changes the direction of an article or a client keeps adding more twists and turns to a project, and I label them "difficult." The truth is I rarely have enough information to make such a judgment; I have only part of a much larger picture. I am not working under the expectations and constraints these people are. In fact, I may not even know what those parameters are. So, since I haven't walked a mile in their moccasins, as an old Indian proverb puts it, I am not in a position to judge. It's that simple.

Can people skills really be as simple as those four rules? If so, why are we not taught those rules early in our lives? Why don't some people ever learn them? I remember reading Robert Fulghum's book, *All I Really Need to Know I Learned*

< 32 >

in Kindergarten, and thinking it should be required reading for every school child. In fact, it is a book for every adult who will ever interact with another person. That would be all of us.

< 33 >

CHAPTER 7

MIND LIKE A SPONGE

mind (mǐnd) *noun*

1. The human consciousness that originates in the brain and is manifested especially in thought, perception, emotion, will, memory, and imagination.
2. The collective conscious and unconscious processes in a sentient organism that direct and influence mental and physical behavior.
3. The principle of intelligence; the spirit of consciousness regarded as an aspect of reality.

sponge (spǔnj) *noun*

1. Absorb, incorporate, engross, assimilate, digest, suck, suck in, soak up, mop up, blot, dry.
2. Internalize, take in, ingest, ingurgitate, imbibe.
3. A primitive sedentary aquatic invertebrate that extracts nutrients and oxygen from water.

What does it mean to have a mind like a sponge? To me, it means a lust for learning and the ability to absorb and retain what is learned. People with such minds see life as "earth school": a huge classroom in which to take in as much as possible; think about it; talk about it; write about it; and, especially, make new and original connections out of it. They are inherently smart, in my experience, though not

< 34 >

always in conventional ways. They may not necessarily belong to Mensa, have a college degree, or even have much formal schooling. On the other hand, they may be very well educated, well traveled, and well versed in the classics. The important thing is that *they know things*. And they know them because they observe life, they question, they listen, they read, and they treat each new piece of knowledge as if it were something of great value.

Whether they are left-brained scientists or mathematicians or right-brained artists or actors, they share an insatiable curiosity about virtually everything. Such people seem incapable of boredom, finding the most prosaic, seemingly dull subjects worthy of attention. Some are introverted and keep all of this information to themselves; others will talk your ear off, convinced that everyone wants to know more.

Their other trait is the ability to integrate all of this information—make it a part of themselves, tuck it away for future reference, and invariably pull it out at exactly the right moment. It's a remarkable gift and quite an indispensable one for a writer. The question is, if you weren't born with this kind of mind, how do you build one from scratch? Here are some ways to begin.

- **Decide to be interested,** even if, at first, you are not. If that is too much, at least decide to be *present*. If you are fully awake and aware, something is bound to strike a chord. If nothing does, you might want to rethink your decision to be a writer. If you are absolutely unable to kindle a flicker of interest, consider that a red flag. Perhaps

< 35 >

you are in the wrong profession or the wrong segment of the right profession.

- **Listen—really listen**—to what your resource person is telling you. Ask questions. Feed back what you think you heard. Don't be satisfied with superficial answers. Dig a little deeper. Engage yourself in a dialogue, rather than a question and answer session, where you throw out a question, the interviewee throws back an answer, and there is no real connection.

- **Think of the assignment as a giant jigsaw puzzle,** with every new piece of information adding to the pattern. Begin to form a diagram in your mind, or on paper, of how the pieces seem to be fitting. Try to picture the puzzle complete, and ask yourself, "What's missing? What do I need to fill in the holes? Where or how can I find it? What will this look like when it's finished?"

- **Play detective.** Look for clues that will lead you to sources that will answer questions or suggest the questions when you don't know what to ask. Nose around. Go to the library. Surf the Net. Seek out experts. Check out websites. Find a unique twist. Follow offbeat leads. Be persistent. Amazing things will happen. You may even get hooked on the topic.

< 36 >

CHAPTER 8

MIND LIKE A MACINTOSH

or·gan·ize (ôr´ge-nìz˝) *verb* or·gan·ized, or·gan·iz·ing,
or·gan·iz·es *verb, transitive*
1. To put together into an orderly, functional,
structured whole.
2. To arrange in a coherent form; systematize:
organized her thoughts before speaking.
3. To arrange in a desired pattern or structure:
*"The painting is organized around a young
reaper enjoying his noonday rest."*
(William Carlos Williams).
4. To arrange systematically for harmonious or united
action: *organize a strike.*

mind (mìnd) *noun*
1. The human consciousness that originates in the brain
and is manifested especially in thought, perception,
emotion, will, memory, and imagination.
2. The collective conscious and unconscious processes
in a sentient organism that direct and influence
mental and physical behavior.
3. The principle of intelligence; the spirit of consciousness regarded as an aspect of reality.
4. The faculty of thinking, reasoning, and applying
knowledge: *Follow your mind, not your heart.*

< 37 >

I hope Windows users will not take offense at the title of this chapter, but, in truth, it *was* Macintosh that invented double-clicking on little folders to retrieve files and documents. Before that creative breakthrough, maneuvering around computer directories was (in my view) a nightmare. I was rarely in the right directory, and if by chance I was, I couldn't remember the name of the file. The Mac, on the other hand, seemed so logical, so user-friendly, and so *organized*. To me, it was and remains a metaphor for how a freelance writer must be able to quickly put her hands on exactly what she needs, when she needs it—be that a file, an invoice, a scrap of paper with a phone number on it, a business card, a memo, or draft #2 of something that is now in its fifth incarnation.

I have ceased to be amazed at clients' expectations. The phone rings, and occasionally the client actually identifies himself. Usually, though, he just starts talking as if we were in the middle of a meeting and he had merely paused to take a sip of coffee. "You know that third paragraph?" he might say. "I think it needs some work. How about if we said it this way?" And he begins to ramble or restate or dictate.

In the meantime, unless I have a system that allows me to reach for the file *as* he is saying hello, grab the appropriate piece of paper, and get to the third paragraph at about the same time he does, I am immediately lost in space. A variation on that theme suggests that I am sitting at the computer, and, no matter what I happen to be doing at the time, I can instantly find and open the client's file, the project file, and the document he is already busily rewriting. Both are

< 38 >

possible, of course, but my goal is to be able to do one or the other with lightning speed. When the client says, "You know that third paragraph…?" I want to be able to reply, "Yes, I'm looking at it right now." Now, *that's* organized!

Is that possible? Yes, believe it or not, it is. Can *I* do it? Sometimes, but not as often as I would like. That's not because I don't know how; it's because I get lazy or sloppy or overwhelmed and let my desk and files get completely out of control. If you're in business, you *have* to be organized. If you're not, you're going to come across as an amateur at best and a creative flake at worst. If the client or editor gets frustrated enough at your inability to deliver in what she considers a timely manner, you can be sure she will go off in search of a "professional."

That's one reason to bring order to chaos in your office. Another is that when you can't find something you need, your stress level skyrockets out of control, which can translate into anything from headaches to stomachaches, from low-back pain to low resistance, from hyperventilating to hives. Your job is tough enough already. This is one headache you can actually prevent, and here is a process to help you do it.

First, take a good hard look at your office. Is it organized? Could you find something if you needed to? Never mind finding it in a split second. Could you find it at all? If not, why not? Is your file system a mess, assuming you have a system? Are there piles of things here, there, and everywhere; an overstuffed things-to-do box; a stack of filing you never seem to get to; research that is so old it is obsolete; files for clients

< 39 >

you don't have anymore; or publications that are out of print? In other words, are you buried in a sea of useless paper?

If so, you are probably overwhelmed with the prospect of bringing order to chaos. That's not unusual; but unless you take a week or two off to do it, there is little hope that you will ever dig out on your own. Here is what you would have to do:

- Go through *every* piece of paper, and act on it, file it, read it, or pitch it.
- Go through *every* file folder, consolidate those you want to keep, and ruthlessly toss the rest. If you're really ambitious, you can recycle the paper.
- Revamp or reorganize your filing system so that it makes sense, not only to you, but also to the imaginary secretary you dream of hiring.
- Clean off your desk and any other surface that has anything on it. That definitely includes the floor.
- Remove anything from your work area that isn't necessary for work, such as non-work related books, knickknacks, excess photos, and general clutter. Put the things you use often within arm's reach.
- Arrange current project files in alphabetical order, and put them close enough to grab when the phone rings. Review their contents so you know what is in each file without shuffling through it frantically.
- Put a long enough cord on the phone to allow you to keep talking if you have to move away from the desk.

< 40 >

Better still, use a portable phone. Best of all, use a battery-powered headset, so your hands stay free.

- If the thought of tackling all of the above makes you physically sick, hire a professional organizational expert. This is not an extravagance; it is an investment in your ability to function.
- Finally, make sure your "system," whatever it may be, works for you. It must be able to grow with you and your business.

Organizing your physical environment is step one; step two is doing the same thing with your computer environment. This could require a chapter all its own, but the fundamental rules are much the same as those for your office.

- Ask yourself, what is cluttering up your computer? What do you really not need? If you can't bear to part with something, back it up in a file called Archive. If you don't need a file or folder, throw it in the trash or recycle bin on your desktop.
- Organize your computer files the same way you have organized your paper files—logically and accessibly.
- Buy a reputable client-management program; enter your clients' or editors' information; keep your records up-to-date; and, before you make a call, review your previous notes.
- If this part is too overwhelming, hire a computer guru to help. It's another very sound investment.

< 41 >

The payoff for all this effort and time? Among the many obvious benefits of an orderly mind, computer, and work area is the biggest benefit of all: When the client or editor calls and begins talking as if you had the file in your hand or on your screen, *you will!*

< 42 >

CHAPTER 9

INTERVIEWING SKILLS

in·ter·view (în´ter-vu) *noun*
1. A conversation, such as one conducted by a reporter, in which facts or statements are elicited from another.
2. An account or a reproduction of such a conversation.

skill (skill) *noun*
1. Proficiency, facility, or dexterity that is acquired or developed through training or experience. See synonyms for ability.
2. An art, a trade, or a technique, particularly one requiring use of the hands or body.
3. A developed talent or ability: *writing skills.*

For me, the heart of research has always been the ability to elicit information from others. For years, it never occurred to me to go to the library or rummage through magazines or official documents. If I wanted to know about something, I found experts on that subject and tried to crawl inside their minds, to cram everything they would tell me into whatever time they would give me, and to understand things about which I knew absolutely nothing. Sometimes, I knew so little I couldn't even frame a decent question.

< 43 >

In those cases, the first interview was always critical because it was the one that provided me with the big picture, key contacts, and politically correct language. This person had to be someone who wouldn't mind that I knew nothing, someone who would be willing to explain the subject from the ground up. I was always amazed at the number of people who met those criteria. After the first interview, I went from one expert to another, asking each of them to refer me to the next, until all of these fragments began to make sense. The whole process was like putting together a giant jigsaw puzzle without a picture of what it would look like when it was completed. Every assignment was a mystery to be solved, often with very few clues.

I would ask myself: What is the point of this story? What do I need to know to make that point? Whom should I talk to, and how can I get to that person? What are the right questions to ask? How will I know when I have enough information? Answering those questions was always an adventure in starting with nothing and watching bits and pieces grow and take shape until they became an article.

Little by little, I was learning the art of interviewing, and, over the years, the ability to do it well has proved to be one of my most valuable strengths. The whole idea of interviewing seems so simple to people. After all, what is it but asking questions? The more I sought and gathered information in this way, the greater my respect for the interviewing process became. It does involve asking questions, of course, but that is only part of what it takes to be an excellent interviewer.

< 44 >

- **First, I believe interviewing requires the courage to take risks.** It is risky to be in the presence of an expert when you can barely pronounce the name of his or her subject, let alone discuss it intelligently. It is risky to admit how little you know and still get this person to talk to you, to teach you everything you need to know, and often to do it in the simplest language possible. It is risky to believe you can then write about such a topic credibly, accurately, and understandably, so that people who know less than you do will understand it and find it interesting.

- **Second, it takes the ability to get your ego out of the way.** You must become virtually invisible so that the spotlight is on your expert, not on you. If you are conscious of yourself, of the questions you are asking, of how you are coming across, of whether the other person thinks you are smart or clever, or of needing to prove how much you know, you have missed the point completely. *An interview isn't about you;* it's about the other person. It's about what that person knows or has experienced or can share with you that will add to your understanding of your topic.

- **Third, you have to be able to take in and process information on the spot.** You do not have the luxury of poring over your notes or listening to your tape at a later time and framing the questions you would ask *after* you have had a chance to review them. You must assume that this is your only chance to ask and that each question or comment will expand your grasp of the subject matter.

< 45 >

That presupposes that, when the other person is talking, you are listening—fully engaged in the content, the nuances, the direction in which he or she is going. You have to be able to capture the message, read between the lines for nonverbal cues, check the accuracy of your understanding, integrate the new information into what you already know, and be prepared to build on that with your next question.

- **Finally, it takes the rare trait of empathy.** Empathy is the ability to feel what the other person is feeling; to capture her enthusiasm for the subject; to view it as she does; and, beyond that, to transmit those feelings through the words you write to the printed page so that they are still alive when the reader finally sees them. Unlike many of the learnable skills of interviewing, empathy is very subtle and can only be cultivated over time.

As a freelance writer, you will encounter many subjects in which you have little interest and more than a few that will bore you to tears. How do you bring such subjects to life? How do you create and sustain interest in something you care nothing about and doubt that the reader will either? The answer is that you find a resource who does care, someone who is very interested in it, who knows a great deal or cares a great deal about it, and who is eager to share what he or she knows with you. And, then, you make those feelings your own.

< 46 >

You purposely set out to capture the other person's excitement, to understand what makes this topic so fascinating. The more questions you ask, the more you learn and, consequently, the better your grasp of the inherent richness of this topic becomes. This ability is not easy to acquire. It doesn't come naturally, especially when you find it difficult to relate to a person or a subject. But if you put aside your own biases and focus on your interviewee's point of view, amazing things happen. Enthusiasm is contagious, and, if you are open and receptive, you can catch it. Empathy is more art than skill, but even art improves with practice.

The test of your interviewing skills is in the finished product. Does it do what it is intended to do: inform, educate, clarify, persuade, amuse, or create a particular impression or feeling? Is it accurate in fact, as well as in tone? Is it honest? Is it alive? Does it sound like the person who actually said these things? Do you understand what you have written, and will your reader? If you do submit it to the interviewee for approval, is it likely to pass muster?

This is the tough test to which you must submit every interview. Even after forty-five years and thousands of interviews, I still ask myself those questions. Just as every piece of writing stands on its own, so does every interview. While it's taking place, you must be 100 percent present—engaged and in the moment. After it's over, you must capture not only its content but also its spirit. And, as you weave it into the fabric of a larger piece of writing, you must work to preserve its integrity.

< 47 >

CHAPTER 10

BUSINESS SENSE

busi·ness (bîz´nîs) *noun*
1. The occupation, work, or trade in which a person is engaged: *the wholesale food business.*
2. A specific occupation or pursuit: *the best designer in the business.*
3. Commercial, industrial, or professional dealings: *new systems now being used in business.*
4. A commercial enterprise or establishment: *bought his uncle's business.*
5. Volume or amount of commercial trade: *Business had fallen off.*

sense (sèns) *noun*
1. Intuitive or acquired perception or ability to estimate: *a sense of diplomatic timing.* a.) A capacity to appreciate or understand: *a keen sense of humor.* b.) A vague feeling: *a sense of impending doom.* c.) Recognition or perception, either through the senses or through the intellect; consciousness: *has no sense of shame.*
2. Normal ability to think or reason soundly; use correct judgment.

< 48 >

In *The E Myth Revisited: Why Most Small Businesses Don't Work and What To Do About It,* consultant and author Michael E. Gerber observes that the real reason people start businesses is not because they are entrepreneurs but because they have been stricken with what he calls an "entrepreneurial seizure." Suddenly, they begin asking themselves, "Why work for somebody else? Why not just work for myself? At least I'll have a nice boss and great working conditions." So, they take the plunge, based on what Gerber calls "the fatal assumption," i.e., "If you understand the technical work of a business, you understand a business that does that technical work."

Apparently, that is rarely the case. Writers understand the technical side of the business because, essentially, we are *technicians*—creators, doers—and we are happiest when we are doing. At least, that is true in my case. When we do decide to make writing a full-time occupation, no matter how well prepared we seem to be, for many of us, it is no less than a seismic shock to discover that, if *we* don't find the work, keep track of and service the clients, send out invoices, collect the money, do the marketing, pay the bills, buy the supplies, and all the other "stuff" that must be done, *no one does it.* The buck really does stop here.

At first, that may seem to be a bit of an adventure—a growth experience—but after a while, all that growing gets exhausting. Personally, I would rather *not* do most of what one *must* do to be in business. All I ever wanted to do was write, and that's what I thought being in business was going to be about. Wrong. Sometimes, it seems that being "in

< 49 >

business" is about everything *but* writing. It's more about keeping it all together, returning phone calls, going through the mail, organizing files, chewing my nails over unpaid client invoices and the resulting unpaid bills, wading through daily emails, learning new software, reconciling my checkbooks (for separate accounts), making sure there is money for estimated quarterly taxes, and on and on and on. If there is time after that, I write.

This is neither a unique problem nor one that is exclusive to writers. It's the universal lament of many creative people and other technicians who experience that proverbial "entrepreneurial seizure" and act on it. The choice faced by those of us who want to become full-time independent writers is this: We can *survive* by clinging to our identity as writers and somehow managing to stay afloat, or we can *thrive* by becoming savvy business owners, as well as top-flight, professional writers. Many freelancers opt for the former, insisting that they just don't have the requisite business sense to be entrepreneurs.

It's true that not all of us are born with it, but business acumen is *not* quantum physics. It can be acquired, nurtured, and expanded. If you truly want to be a successful, independently employed writer, you have no choice. The question now becomes, where and how do you begin? Here are a few fairly painless suggestions:

- **Start with an attitude adjustment.** Running your business as a business is certainly not as bad as cleaning out a hopelessly cluttered basement or finally getting started on

< 50 >

your income taxes the night before they are due. In the first place, it is an essential part of earning a living. In the second, if you are smart enough to be a writer, you are smart enough to run your own show. Even if the business side of the business is not your strong suit or your preference, that doesn't mean you're not capable of handling it. So, your new attitude should incorporate these assertions: *I am a professional writer **and** an entrepreneur. I know that my ultimate success depends on mastery of both aspects of my business, and I am going to excel in both roles.*

- **If you don't already have one, hire an accountant.** There are things you can do and should do; and there are other things that will eat up your time, zap your energy, and create needless stress. Taking care of every single aspect of your finances, from paying your bills to filing your taxes, is not necessary. Decide what you must do yourself and what you can comfortably delegate. I would like to delegate everything, but I can't afford a full-time bookkeeper/accountant yet. When I can, believe me, I will hire one.

- **Master the basics.** Make a list of what has to be done that you are not doing or don't want to do. If you're not sure what you should be doing, buy a book, take a business course, or ask your accountant. Admit that there are things you don't know, and learn how to do them. When you bought your first computer, chances are you were not

< 51 >

an expert. When you start a business, unless you've done it before, you will definitely have a lot to learn. You can't operate with only a manual typewriter in today's technologically sophisticated environment, and you can't run a professional operation on a wing and a prayer.

- **Make time to wear your business hat.** It can be maddening to do all the things that must be done when you have assignments and deadliness, but the business will not run itself. Carve out a particular time to put the administrative side of the business in order. Send invoices on time, and resend them on their due dates if they have not been paid. Keep up to date on record keeping. Client management, time and billing, check writing, and scheduling programs all speed up and simplify these essential tasks.

The E Myth is seductive. But the word "myth" is important. It is simply not true that, if you understand the technical work of a business, you understand a business that does that technical work. Writing an article or a newsletter or even a book is something you have learned to do over time; running an efficient, profitable, growing business requires a whole new learning curve.

< 52 >

CHAPTER 11

ENDURANCE & PHYSICAL STAMINA

en·dur·ance (èn-dur´ens, -dyur´-) *noun*
1. The act, quality, or power of withstanding hardship or stress: *A marathon tests a runner's endurance.*
2. The state or fact of persevering: *Through hard work and endurance, we will complete this project.*
3. Continuing existence; duration.

stam·i·na (stàm´e-ne) *noun*
Physical or moral strength to resist or withstand illness, fatigue, or hardship; endurance.

Writing is an extremely physical activity—something that never occurred to me when I started out. Forty-five years ago, we didn't have computers; we were lucky to have electric typewriters. Mine was a little blue Smith Corona portable. I couldn't afford an IBM Self-Correcting Selectric, which I coveted for years. I remember the feel of my fingers on the keys, tripping all over themselves; the sound of the bell that indicated the end of a line; and shoving the carriage so hard I thought one day it would fall off. Most of all, I remember *sitting* for hours on end.

< 53 >

I took great pride in being able to sit for up to twelve hours at a time, refusing to abandon my post until I finished whatever I was writing. By the time I did finish, I was in a pretzel knot from hunching over the typewriter, but I refused to give in. It was an endurance contest I always won, though, for the life of me, I don't remember how I did it or why it seemed so important.

Typewriters, of course, are now as obsolete as carbon paper, and the life of a writer supposedly has been made much easier by all of this fabulous technology. After all, we don't have to white out, correct, retype, pick up all that discarded typewriter paper, or half the things we used to do. The life of a writer should be a breeze. Yet, strangely, I find my work much more tiring than I used to.

It's a given that I've lived a few decades since those twelve-hour days and that my hands have lost much of their former dexterity. But those things don't really explain the fatigue that is somehow different in nature from the "just plain pooped" I used to experience. Some of it is eye strain from staring endlessly at little type on a glaring screen; some of it is repetitive-motion pain because my hands and wrists seem to be doing the same things over and over again in a different way than when they hit typewriter keys; and some of it is the ergonomically incorrect height of my chair or my keyboard, how my back is or isn't supported, and on and on. The bottom line is that writers ought to join a gym or hire a personal trainer just to stay in shape to do what we do for a living.

< 54 >

Actually, I'm serious. Exercise is absolutely essential for those of who spend so much of our time on our derriéres, hunched over a keyboard, totally focused on stringing words across a computer screen. Why? Because it develops stamina, strength, and flexibility; clears the mind, calms the soul, and relieves stress; jump starts the creative process; releases endorphins; and brings balance to a highly cerebral vocation. It also feels good—for some of us, while we're doing it; for others, when we stop doing it. In any case, regular physical exercise should be mandatory.

Stamina and endurance apply to our minds as well as our bodies. In the kind of work that requires high-functioning mental and creative processes, no writer can afford fog on the brain. And that is a real danger when you're tired or stressed or have been working on the same thing for too many hours. How do you know when you are on mental overload and your brain has shut down? For one thing, there are physical clues. It may be a headache or the feeling that your head is swimming. Your eyes may refuse to focus or just close. You may begin to make more than your usual number of typing errors.

Equally important, yet more difficult to recognize, are the mental symptoms: Your concentration begins to slip, and writing becomes more of a rock slide than a flowing stream (I know, for many people it is *always* a rock slide). You may lose your place or your enthusiasm. For me, the "knowing" comes when I realize that my writing has become *mechanical*. The minute I become aware of that, I stop, even if it's in mid-sentence.

< 55 >

Physical exercise is a tuneup for the mind as much as for the body. It is rejuvenating, refreshing, and relaxing, all at the same time. There are many other ways to give your brain a rest, including listening to music, getting a good dose of nature, drawing or painting, cleaning the house, walking the dog, meditating, doing yoga or stretching, taking a nap, or simply staring into space. For most of us, *doing nothing* is the hardest thing in the world, but often that's all it takes to blow the fog away.

You need endurance and stamina to sit for hours, stay alert, and write well. It sounds prosaic, but the best advice is what you've heard a thousand times: eat a healthy diet, exercise regularly, get adequate sleep, and try to bring balance to your life. Your creativity and livelihood depend on it.

< 56 >

CHAPTER 12

FOCUS & ATTENTION SPAN

at·ten·tion (e-tèn´shen) *noun*
1. Concentration of the mental powers upon an object; a close or careful observing or listening.
2. The ability or power to concentrate mentally.

attention span *noun*
The length of time during which a person can concentrate or focus attention on a particular object or idea without diversion.

fo·cus (fo´kes) *noun*
1. Pay some attention, glance at, look into.
2. Be attentive, attend, give attention, pay attention.
3. Devote or give one's attention to, direct one's thoughts to, think.
4. Rivet one's attention to, concentrate on.
5. Examine, inspect, scrutinize, vet, review, pass under review, scan, study closely, pore, mull, read, reread, digest, study.

< 57 >

Some types of writing can be achieved in a relatively short time span. In advertising, for example, the bulk of a writer's effort goes on *before* the writing begins. Like an iceberg, hidden from view, the brainstorming and creative processes are unseen and can take more time than the actual act of putting words on paper … or, more accurately, on a computer screen. That part often seems to come in a flash of inspiration. "Eureka, I've got it," and The Pepsi Generation is born.

Such instances are the exception rather than the rule. The rule is that most writing takes time—lots of time. An article, a brochure, an annual report, a speech, a training program, a website, and certainly, a book are not conceived in a single brainstorming session or written in a matter of hours. Any of them, as well as many other assignments a freelance writer is likely to encounter, may consume weeks, at least, and many months at most.

Of the myriad strengths a writer needs, two of the most important are focus and a long attention span. Focus means total concentration or fixed attention on the project at hand. The above definition suggests that you are also very interested in this activity. You are immersed in the subject, to the point that you are almost one with it. It helps if you are one of those people who is incapable of boredom, because you will be asked to write about many things that would put the average person to sleep. If you're focused, you are, by definition, not bored. The trick is to *stay* focused; that is what is meant by having a long attention span.

The ability to get excited about a subject and stay excited is a rare gift. If you weren't born with this talent, I would do what you can to cultivate it.

< 58 >

There are a number of prescribed steps to putting together a good feature article, no matter what kind of publication it will appear in. The steps begin with the initial assignment and end with a final, approved manuscript. In between, there is the need to track down sources, conduct interviews and all other varieties of research; sort, absorb, and process the information you have gathered; write a first draft; spell check, revise, proofread, refine, do a final edit, rewrite; and, at last, send it off to the editor.

That's the *best*-case scenario. The *worst*-case scenario is when the editor or client wants it shorter, longer, more detailed, or completely different from the way you wrote it. At that point, you may find yourself back at square one, virtually starting over. In either case, it can be a real challenge to keep your interest and enthusiasm from waning or just plain dying. The secret lies in your *attitude*—the one element over which you have complete control.

Attitude is a conscious choice. *You* create it, *you* nurture it, *you* keep it alive through every step of the process, no matter how long it takes or how frustrated you may become. Here are the attitudes I have cultivated over time about each of the steps in the process.

- **Initial assignment:** a way to add to my store of knowledge or to learn something completely new
- **Tracking down sources:** a timed scavenger hunt
- **Interviews, research:** assembling a complicated puzzle
- **Sort, absorb, and process:** cramming for an exam (believe it or not, I *enjoyed* that)

< 59 >

- **First draft:** a state of "flow," to borrow the words of psychologist and author Mihaly Csikszentmihalyi
- **Revising, refining, rewriting:** going for the gold
- **Sending it off:** satisfaction, confidence, and relief
- **Great reviews:** sometimes, even better than money
- **Not-so-great reviews:** gratitude (honest!) for an opportunity to improve the product
- **Back to square one:** another chance to perfect the process (this is the tough one)

Does it really work? Most of the time, it does. Choosing the most productive attitude at each step of the process keeps me focused for as long as necessary. In a project like an annual report, that could be several months; for a book, it could be well over a year. As I said, it helps to be incapable of boredom.

< 60 >

CHAPTER 13

MARKETING SAVVY

Mar·ket·ing (mär´kî-tîng) *noun*
1. The act or process of buying and selling in a market.
2. The commercial functions involved in transferring goods from producer to consumer.
3. The ability to perceive a need in the marketplace and find a unique way to fill it.

Sav·vy (sàv´ê) *informal. Adjective/noun*
1. Well informed and perceptive; shrewd.
2. Practical understanding or shrewdness: *a banker known for financial savvy.*

Few words are as misunderstood and misused as the word *marketing.* It seems that no matter what the activity—from sales to public relations to telephone solicitation—it is called marketing. Even the above definitions are not precisely accurate. Marketing does *not* mean selling; it means identifying a need in the market place and finding a way to fill it. As it applies to surviving and thriving as a free-lance writer, marketing means letting potential clients or editors know who you are, how you can help them, and why you should be the first and only person they call. If people don't know who you are or what you can do for them, you

< 61 >

are hardly going to be the first person they think of when they need help.

It's all a matter of attitude. When you have a marketing mindset, you are always asking yourself, what is the problem and how can I help solve it? Since every problem is unique, there is no such thing as a one-size-fits-all solution. Therefore, your solution must be custom-tailored to each problem. The better your investigative technique and problem-solving skills, the more likely you are to land the assignment and to build ongoing credibility. To stand out from your competitors, you need to have marketing savvy. To develop it, adopt the following behaviors and actions.

- **Think of life as a marketing call.** Believe it; live it. Realize that every single thing you do or say is an element of your personal marketing strategy. "Everything" includes the quality of your work; your attitude, appearance, and demeanor; the message on your voice mail and how quickly you return calls; your marketing materials and how well they demonstrate your ability to communicate; samples of your work and the way you present those samples; and all the ways in which you interact with the world.

- **Set aside a certain number of hours a day or each week for marketing.** Make them sacrosanct. Don't say, "That's a great idea, but I'm too busy working." Remember all those times when busy-ness gave way to nothingness

< 62 >

and you kicked yourself for failing to fill the pipeline. Don't kick yourself; take time and make time to market yourself and your business.

- **Take your own advice.** Do for yourself what you would advise your clients to do. They are paying you to help them get their message across, and you are telling them all the best ways to do it. What about *your* message? If your recommendations work for others, won't they work equally well for you? Write down your advice to your clients; then scratch out their company name, and write in your own. If all else fails, pretend you hired a marketing consultant to help you.

- **Network.** Attend networking events. Do face time; pass out business cards; collect business cards; follow up with phone calls or notes. If life is indeed a marketing call, networking events are golden opportunities to meet people, to determine what they may need and how you could supply it, to make a good impression, and to let them know enough about you to want to know more.

- **Join organizations and get involved.** Carefully select the organizations you join, and play an active role in their activities. The possibilities are vast. You can choose among professional, civic, trade or industry, charitable, and small-business groups. But before you sign your application form, ask yourself these three questions: Does

< 63 >

the focus of this group interest me? Can I grow professionally and personally from my involvement? Are those who belong people I want to know or who could further my business goals?

- **Solicit referrals from satisfied clients or editors.** If you have done a good job and your work is valued, ask if there is someone else to whom your clients or editors might refer you. If you aren't asking for referrals yet, start now. Every satisfied customer has an address book full of contacts. Even one name will provide a valuable lead.

- **Think outside the box.** Get involved in activities that put you outside of your comfort zone. Most of us have unexplored areas in our lives—things we have thought about doing but have never taken the time to do. There are two good reasons to try this: First, it will expand your horizons, and you might have fun; second, it will put you in proximity to people you would not ordinarily meet.

- **Create a website; then promote it.** The Internet is a mighty presence in our lives, and it is increasingly important to have a presence on the Web. If you are in communications and you want to get your name out there in cyberspace, a website is one way to do it. But (there is always a but), if you do launch your own site, know what you hope to accomplish; do it well or hire someone to do it well for you; consult an SEO expert; register it with

< 64 >

beaucoup directories; change it or update it frequently; and promote it, promote it, promote it. A website can be effective, or it can be a frivolous and extravagant exercise in feeding your ego.

- **Be your own PR person.** No one knows better than you do how good you are. No one else has such a vested interest in your success. No one can tell your story as well as you can. So why not put all those ingredients together and mount your own PR campaign? If you believe in the product—as well you should—no one can sell it as well as you can.

< 65 >

CHAPTER 14

TECHNICAL COMPETENCE

tech·ni·cal (tèk´nî-kel) *adjective*
1. Of, relating to, or derived from technique.
2. a.) Having special skill or practical knowledge especially in a mechanical or scientific field: *a technical adviser.* b.) Used in or peculiar to a specific field or profession; specialized: *technical terminology.*
3. Belonging or relating to a particular subject: *technical expertise.*
4. According to principle; formal rather than practical: *a technical advantage.*
5. Industrial and mechanical; *technological.*

com·pe·tence (kòm´pî-tens) *noun*
1. The state or quality of being adequately or well qualified; ability. See synonyms for *ability.*
2. A specific range of skill, knowledge, or ability.

It is virtually impossible to be a full-time freelance writer without being computer literate. Moreover, it is becoming impossible to sustain yourself in this business unless you are online, with email, both at home and away. It goes without saying that you have a smart phone or an iPhone, a laptop, and fax capabilities on your computer. You may also own a scanner/copy machine/printing device, an external hard

< 66 >

drive or a "cloud" back-up system, and countless software programs.

If you are at the stage of merely *contemplating* going into business, that list may seem daunting. First, there is the cost; second, there is the necessity to *set up and use* all of that can't-live-without equipment. When I started my business twenty-five years ago, some of that technology didn't even exist, or, if it did, it wasn't absolutely necessary for survival. What is so astonishing is how much has changed. I have added one piece of equipment at a time over the years because I felt it enabled me to better serve my clients. From one now-extinct Osborne computer and a dot-matrix printer, I have upgraded to the point of having barely any open desk space and a floor full of twisted, overlapping electrical cords. Over time, I have eliminated many pieces of equipment I no longer needed.

Any major corporation that is not set up to compete in the era of e-commerce is at a distinct disadvantage in the 21st century. Like it or not, that is today's reality. While you may never be connected to a WAN (wide area network) or have your clients pay you with credit cards or electronic checks, there are other things that will be expected of you as a businessperson. Here are some steps you should take, if you are to meet those expectations.

- **Upgrade your computer** (or buy a new one) so that it functions at the optimum level for your particular business. That may mean adding more memory, a second external hard drive, or a better back-up system.

< 67 >

- **Check, optimize, de-fragment, and generally clean up your hard drive.** Use trouble-shooting tools or built-in programs to be certain everything is in working order. Be sure your virus detection program is up to date.

- **Clean up your files.** Get rid of the junk or applications you have never used and never will; games that came with the system, especially if you don't play games; and anything else that is taking up space but serving no useful purpose. Back up and archive all of your inactive clients and projects, old research, and infrequently used files; and get them off your hard drive.

- **Back up everything that's left,** including the system, on a separate hard drive, Dropbox, Carbonite, or any system with a cloud. Check with consumerreports.com if you aren't sure which one to use. If that requires special software, buy it. If you've ever had a hard-drive crash, you know it is well worth the investment. If you haven't, there is a 92 percent chance that you will.

- **Make sure your operating system and software are compatible with your clients' or publishers'** or can be reconfigured to interface, if it is not. You may need to make some changes by adding software packages, upgrading your system, or even purchasing a second computer. It used to be pretty much a nightmare to communicate between PCs and Macs, but these days, most software packages can be read by both.

< 68 >

- **Take inventory of your equipment.** What do you have, and what do you need that you don't have? If your clients are aggravated by not being able to send a fax because you are on the phone or the Internet, you need a second phone line. If you don't get messages because your answering machine breaks down or your voice mailbox is on overload, that is a problem you must fix. If everyone is on email and you're still resisting, you are, in effect, cutting yourself off from the world. If you are *out* more than you are *in*, you have to remember to either check your voice mail *every* hour, or have your calls forwarded to your cell phone. The point is to make it easy for others to do business with you in this electronic age.

- **Finally, as you add all of this paraphernalia, learn to use it correctly.** Having all the bells and whistles but not knowing how to make them work for your business does not increase your responsiveness; it just decreases your bank account. The name of the game is not, *he who dies with the most toys wins*; it is, *she who best meets her clients' needs succeeds in business.*

< 69 >

CHAPTER 15

SELF-CONFIDENCE

con·fi·dence (kòn´fĭ-dens) *noun*
1. Trust or faith in a person or thing.
2. The state or quality of being certain: *I have every confidence in your ability to succeed.*
Synonyms: confidence, assurance, aplomb, self-confidence, self-possession. These nouns denote a feeling of emotional security resulting from faith in one's self. *Confidence* is a firm belief in one's powers, abilities, or capacities.

Writers put words on paper for public consumption, and it isn't always easy. Why? Isn't that what we are supposed do? What kind of courage does it take to write something—a piece of news, a brochure, a PR release, or an article—and let someone else read it? How scary could that be? The answers to those questions are: Yes, that *is* what writers do. And, in reality, it takes a great deal of courage to do it time after time; day after day; sometimes, year after year. In fact, there are few aspects of freelance writing that don't require just plain *chutzpah*. Think about what it takes to make a living this way.

< 70 >

- **Finding work:** To get an assignment in the first place writers have to make cold calls, send out query letters, show our work, and prove again and again that we have the experience, ability, and wherewithal to do the job. In short, we are constantly trying out for the part.

- **Proving ourselves:** Once we've gotten over that hurdle, no matter how many years we may have been doing this type of thing, we have to convince the client or editor that we are capable of learning *their* particular business, product, audience, or unique perspective. And then we have to prove it.

- **Pricing our work:** Clients usually want to know what the project is going to cost before we have any idea how much of the information is supplied, how much will have to be researched, how many interviews are required, how long it will take to write a first draft, and how many revisions there are likely to be, for starters. Sometimes, we aren't exactly sure of what the client wants because he or she can't quite articulate it. (*"I'll know it when I see it,"* should be a bright red flag!) Yet, even without this basic information, we are expected to come up with an estimate—and live with it—even if it turns out to be ridiculous.

- **Standing our ground:** When we finally arrive at an hourly or project fee that reflects our experience and expertise, we not only have to say it out loud, we have to mean it and insist on it, even when the client or editor says, "What

< 71 >

makes you worth *that much?* I could hire someone for half that amount!" If we submit a contract or letter of agreement with such terms as, "I will begin this project upon receipt of this agreement and 50 percent of the agreed-upon fee," it takes inordinate self-confidence to sit tight until the agreement is signed and the check is in hand.

- **Learning to leave:** And, finally, when the client or editor turns out to be impossible to work with, satisfy, or respect (but you need the money), think of how gutsy it is to say, "This relationship doesn't seem to be working out to our mutual satisfaction. I believe that you should seek another writer."

These are not unusual scenarios; they come with the territory. To face such challenges to one's self-esteem requires a special brand of confidence—one that is solid and assured but never arrogant or defensive. If you're good, you're good. If you've proved it 10,000 times in every conceivable circumstance, you know it. In fact, you radiate it—or, at least, you should.

An experienced writer I knew was asked by an editor for a sample of his work. He haughtily replied, *"My dear young woman, I do not audition."* Not so. As freelance writers, *we are constantly auditioning.* The trick is to do so with confidence and class. The question then becomes, how does one achieve that attitude?

< 72 >

It would take an entire book to answer that question, and, even then, there is no guarantee that the reader will put the answers into practice and become self-confident. But since this is an issue that particularly plagues writers, and one of the critical traits it takes to succeed, here are some techniques I have found helpful over the years.

- **Give every project your all.** Then, you'll always know you did the best job you could possibly do. That is one of the most powerful confidence builders you can employ.

- **Maintain your professionalism in every situation.** Expect to be treated as a professional. Among other things, that means that you do not have to accept inappropriate or abusive behavior. It takes a strong feeling of self-worth to put a stop to such treatment, even if it means leaving the room or leaving the client, but it's very important to your self-respect to do it.

- **If you're not getting feedback, ask for it.** Writers often feel as if we are throwing our work into a bottomless black hole. A lack of criticism in *not* the same as a compliment or positive reinforcement. It's just a lack of feedback.

- **Take criticism graciously.** Learn from it. Get your ego out of the way, and concentrate on finding the best solution to a communication problem, not on being a star. Consider constructive criticism a way to improve your work.

< 73 >

- **Accept praise.** If you receive a well-deserved pat on the back for a job well done, accept it with appreciation. Often, the best response is a simple, "Thank you."

- **Keep a portfolio of your best work.** That has two purposes: First, it is a powerful marketing tool; second, it reminds you of how good you are.

- **Keep a file of any "fan letters" you receive.** Reread them on bad days. They provide spontaneous, sincere positive reinforcement, which is worth its weight in gold.

Remember that self-confidence in a creative field does not always come naturally. Even if you were born with it, it is subject to rough treatment in this business. That's why it's important to keep it from eroding by reinforcing it after each perceived assault. If you consistently do your best work, you will know it and so will those who hire you. Excellence has a way of shining its own light.

< 74 >

FINDING FOCUS:

How to carve out your niche as a freelance writer

< 75 >

CHAPTER 16

TELEPHOTO OR WIDE-ANGLE LENS

tel·e·pho·to (tèl´e-fo˝to) *adjective*
1. Of or relating to a photographic lens or lens system used to produce a large image of a distant object.
2. Of or relating to an instrument that electrically transmits photographs.
3. A telephoto lens.
4. A photograph made with a telephoto lens; a telephotograph.

wide-an·gle (wìd´àng´gel) *adjective*
Of, having, or being a camera lens with a relatively short focal length that permits an angle of view wider than approximately 70°.

choice (chois) *noun*
1. The act of choosing; selection.
2. The power, right, or liberty to choose; option.
3. One that is chosen.
4. A number or variety from which to choose: *a wide choice of styles and colors.*
5. The best or most preferable option.
6. An alternative.

< 77 >

Using a photographic analogy to make a point about writing is a good way to present one of the toughest decisions you will face as a freelancer: the choice between focusing tightly on a particular area (genre, style, subject, medium) or becoming a generalist who does a little bit of everything. In my own case, I began as a specialist—as a feature writer—and, over the years, evolved into a generalist. The latter wasn't intentional; it was simply the direction in which my work took me. Now that I think about it, the process was backwards. Most writers start out by dabbling in a wide range of disciplines and gradually hone their skills in one or two.

I have always seen a discernible difference between these two approaches. To me, being a generalist is what is required of a communication consultant, business writer, and business owner. My tag line for my business was "helping your organization get its message across." That means whatever the message, whomever the audience, and however possible. The message may vary from telling the world who you are and what you do or announcing a merger to responding to a crisis. The audience might be shareholders, employees, customers, or the public. And the method can run the gamut from video training or employee magazines to annual reports and executive speeches.

That is the nature of my business. Whatever it takes to craft and disseminate a message, that's what I do. My brochure and website contain a litany of messages and media (advertising, annual reports, audio/video, brochures, books, etc.), as well as subject matter and industries (manufacturing, healthcare,

< 78 >

banking and finance, agriculture, universities, not-for-profits, and so forth). It seems audacious to suggest that I can do all of those things and do them well. Admittedly, I do some things better than others, and I enjoy some things more than others. If I feel I am not an expert in something—design or catchy ad copy, for example—I find someone who is, and we work as a team. The persistent, overriding question is, What is the best way to communicate this message? The more I am equipped to do that, the better able I will be to find that best way.

Which choice is the best one? There are as many answers to that question as there are writers. In other words, it is a highly individual decision. On one hand, if you specialize, you can become an expert at one or two things; but as a consequence, you will be limiting yourself. On the other hand, if you try to be all things to all people, you will enjoy tremendous variety and an ongoing education, but you may always feel like a jack-of-all-trades and master of none. The general rule of thumb is to get all of the experience you can in a broad array of disciplines and subject matter, and then narrow your focus to those for which you seem best suited.

To be a generalist, the advice is simple: Whatever comes along, seize the opportunity to learn about it, tackle it, and add it to your growing list of capabilities. You'll be amazed at how fast that list grows. I am the first to admit, this is not an easy route to follow. You will be in a constant learning mode, always feeling just a little uncertain about how much you know or still need to understand.

< 79 >

If you opt to be a specialist, you may find yourself over-whielmed with options. There are so many directions in which to go. If one doesn't work, try something else; or if you find the one you've chosen is too limiting, expand it.

The rest of the chapters in this section explore many of the options available to you. When you are finished reading, you may not have chosen your specialty, but you will certainly have more information on which to base such a choice.

< 80 >

CHAPTER 17

INDUSTRY/SUBJECT

in·dus·try (în´de-strê) *plural* **in·dus·tries:** A specific branch of manufacture and trade: *the textile industry.* See synonyms at *business.*

subject matter *noun:* Matter under consideration in a written work or speech; a theme.

Focusing on a particular industry can be a conscious choice or the result of circumstances. If, for example, your professional or academic background is in science or technology, theater, social services, healthcare, or some other specialized area—and you are a writer—it would certainly make sense to combine two strong suits into one career. On the other hand, if you take a job or accept an assignment in an unfamiliar industry, you will not only learn on the job, you may find that you enjoy what you're learning.

The longer you write about a subject, the more of an expert you become, until one day you realize that you know a great deal about it and that your knowledge is marketable. If your interest persists and you stay in the job (full time or freelance), you will have found your niche. Then, you have two alternatives: You can invest yourself totally in this single area, or you can use it as a launching pad to learn and write

< 81 >

about other related areas. Either way, you are becoming a specialist, which is always a strong foundation on which to build.

There are many advantages to being known as a specialist in a particular subject or an industry, especially when that business segment is "hot." This is the era of technology in all its myriad forms. Technology is an umbrella term for everything from computers to smart phones, high-speed Internet access to cyber fraud. It encompasses a field that is changing so fast it's difficult for most people to keep up.

To specialize in writing about any aspect of technology requires, first, that you understand it and, second, that you can communicate that understanding in language that is appropriate to your target audience. Consider software: If you're writing for "techies," you'd better be one or, at the very least, sound like one.

There's an expected jargon, as there is in every field. You have to speak the language. Conversely, if you're writing for the rest of the world, you must be able to translate complex concepts into the everyday language.

Another advantage of becoming well versed in a particular industry is your marketability. While clients are often willing to invest in letting you learn on the job, they would much prefer to hire a writer who knows their business. The ideal, of course, is to keep building on what you have learned and eventually to be considered an extension of the client's staff. I have several clients who have continued to invest in my education over the years and consider it time and money well spent to get the product they need.

< 82 >

Editors, too, are more likely to accept submissions from subject experts than from writers whose backgrounds are more general. One of the less tangible but most important outgrowths of knowing your stuff is the confidence it gives you. When you're face to face with the CEO or some other high-ranking executive, it's important to know the subject well enough to ask intelligent questions.

While writers can learn about anything we set our minds to, we all know we are better suited to some subjects than to others. To write about technology requires an aptitude for left-brain thinking, i.e., concrete, logical, mathematical, scientific. To write about dance, theater, or any facet of the arts, you would more likely be a right-brained thinker—creative, abstract, intuitive. It's partly a matter of preference and partly a matter of inclination, and they often go hand in hand.

What happens when you find yourself writing about a subject you don't understand or find philosophically abhorrent? Just as we have an affinity for certain subjects, we can have aversions to others. If you're an environmentalist and you are hired to write for a company that is being sued for pollution, what do you do? If you are an advocate for gun control, do you take on the National Rifle Association as a client? If you sincerely believe in cultural diversity and tolerance, and your client or editor routinely makes racial slurs, do you resign? These are not far-fetched examples; while they don't occur every day, they may well be the type of choices you will face from time to time.

< 83 >

There is no simple, absolutely correct answer to any of those questions, any more than there are to many of life's dilemmas. The choice is always yours to make, but you do have the right to walk away. One of the joys of freelancing is the freedom to take on the assignments or clients you enjoy and to say "no thank you" to those that just don't feel right. In a world in which we are so often expected to compromise, this is one place you don't have to.

< 84 >

CHAPTER 18

MARKETING COMMUNICATIONS

mar·ket·ing (mär´kî-tǐng) *noun*
1. The act or process of buying and selling in a market.
2. The commercial functions involved in transferring goods from producer to consumer.

com·mu·ni·ca·tions (ke-my͞oŏ´nĭ-kā´shens) *noun*
1. The act of communicating or transmitting a message.
2. The exchange of thoughts, messages, or information, as by speech, signals, writing, or behavior.
3. A means of communicating via a network of routes for sending messages.
4. The technology employed in transmitting messages.

Marketing is a word with several interpretations, depending on its context. Technically, it means perceiving a need in the marketplace and finding a way to fill it. Typically, however, it is used as a synonym for sales. In the context of this chapter, it is all of the ways in which an organization communicates the right message to the right audience through the right media.

Successful marketing begins with a well-conceived plan that includes a number of specialized areas. Ideally, these areas complement each other and work together to produce a cohesive program. The most common vehicles for getting

< 85 >

a message across are public relations (PR), advertising, direct mail, special events, point-of-purchase displays, packaging, website copy and premiums. For freelance writers, the ones to focus on are public relations, advertising, and direct mail, because all three depend on the written word.

PR is a complex field in itself, comprised of a number of disciplines. A well-rounded public relations professional must, first and foremost, be an excellent writer. But it doesn't hurt to be an expert—or, at the very least, competent—in media relations, event planning, client service, and crisis communications, as well.

PR agencies come in all sizes, from one-man bands to influential, international mega-firms. But the agency route is not the only option for talented writers. Almost all significant corporations have at least one PR professional and, more often, an entire department dedicated to framing their messages and trying to control how they are disseminated. One of PR's weaknesses is that such control often slips away when the message is edited on its way to press, written by a staff writer, or interpreted by the print or electronic media. Its greatest strength, on the other hand, is that the message usually comes wrapped in an aura of credibility.

In advertising, the company—through its own staff, an ad agency, or a freelancer—maintains total control over every aspect of its message, from what it says and how it is presented to what vehicle is chosen as its launching pad. But because everyone knows an ad or a commercial is created by professionals and paid for by the client or corporation, neither may be as readily believed as an article or testimonial

< 86 >

from a satisfied customer. Advertising copywriters must be deductive thinkers who can take a five-hundred-word message and boil it down to a pithy headline that sticks in your brain. Since I am better able to take a headline and write five hundred words about it, this kind of writing is not my first choice.

The purpose of direct mail is to have it jump out of the bottomless pile of mail the addressee receives every day, grab that person's attention, and create enough interest to actually have her open and read it. Just think of the pile of "junk mail" you have to wade through and where it usually ends up, and you'll know how daunting an assignment this can be. Direct-mail copy has to be catchy and compelling, but if your wonderful words aren't packaged in a way that stands out from the crowd, they will end up in the trash. Whether direct mail is a personal letter; a mass-mailed, multi-piece grouping with a self-addressed tear-off card; or a clever box with a surprise inside, it takes a special kind of creative mind to write the copy.

How do you decide which route to take? If you can, try all three. You won't really know where your strengths lie or which style gets your creative juices flowing until you plunge in. Even if you decide to specialize in marketing communications, it's a very broad term that requires several different kinds of writing styles. It never hurts to expand your horizons. In fact, it's a very good idea if you are hoping for a long and fruitful career as a freelance writer.

< 87 >

CHAPTER 19

FINANCIAL COMMUNICATIONS

fi·nan·cial (fe-nàn´shel, fĭ-) *adjective*
Of, relating to, or involving finance, finances,
or financiers.

com·mu·ni·ca·tions (ke-my¡˝nî-kâ´shens) *noun*
1. The act of communicating; transmission.
    a.) The exchange of thoughts, messages, or informa-
    tion, as by speech, signals, writing, or behavior;
    b.) Interpersonal rapport; c.) communications *(used
    with a sing. or pl. verb)*. The art and technique of
    using words effectively and with grace in imparting
    one's ideas.
2. Something communicated; a message.

I am not a numbers person. In fact, I would describe
myself as numerically challenged. If I'm in the presence of a
discussion on a mathematical or financial topic, I tend to
zone out. If I'm reading something and happen upon
numbers, my eyes just slide right by them. I have even been
known to become physically ill when forced to think about
my own finances. I am not proud of this rather obvious flaw,
especially since I am a business writer. "Do you write annual
reports?" a prospective client will ask me. "Of course," I
reply; and, in fact, that is true. I do write annual reports.

< 88 >

How is that possible, given my antipathy toward numbers? I can only say that, while it is possible, it *is* certainly not an ideal situation. Knowing that, I have been battling this weakness for many years. When I first began to write, I dealt with just about every subject under the sun *but* finance. I wrote about the arts, medicine, education, construction, manufacturing, fashion, transportation, retirement, politics, alcoholism, and even transcendental meditation. I thought of myself as a magazine journalist, rather than a business writer, even though I worked for a business publication. There seemed no reason to delve into financial writing, so I didn't.

Even when I moved into corporate communications, I wrote only around the edges of financial subjects, so it remained a non-issue. It was only when I launched my own business that I was forced to face the demon. Since I have little background in math and none in accounting or economics, it has required sheer determination on my part. I force myself to read the *St. Louis Business Journal*, the business section of *The New York Times*, and the important business magazines. I fight my way through books on basic finance and investing, and I interview all of the financial gurus who will talk to me, always asking them to define terms they assume I know. It is hardly an ego trip, but it is something I must do. In fact, I should be doing a great deal more.

I interviewed a vice president of investor relations and financial communications, who explained what it takes to make it in this field. Apparently, it takes years of study, effort,

< 89 >

on-the-job training, and practice. At this stage in my career, while I can and will continue to learn and improve, I cannot hope to become a bona fide "expert." However, if I were just beginning to build my repertoire of skills, I would do things differently. So, based on what I did not do and the observations of an expert who did it all, here are some suggestions for making financial communications a viable possibility.

- If fear of numbers or dollar signs is standing in your way, you have two choices: Conquer the fear, or forget about going into this area of writing. Conquering the fear, while difficult, is possible. People overcome phobias all the time. If you really want to do this, you can. One way is to stick a toe in the water and tackle the subject one step at a time. Another is to plunge in and just go for it, no matter how uncomfortable you may feel at the beginning.

- While you can get into financial communications from some very unlikely places, by accident, or the demands of the job, it is far better to do it intentionally. Learning on the fly is certainly possible, but in an area as technical as this one, learning intentionally is preferable. Take an accounting course, read books on finance and investing, talk to people who understand or work in the field. The more you explore, the clearer you will become on what you need to learn, and the more directed your education will become.

< 90 >

- No matter what topic you tackle, chances are you have to become fluent in its jargon, even if you write in plain English. Finance is no different. It has its own language and you can learn it by taking courses, reading everything from *The Wall Street Journal* to the financial sections of annual reports, or having a CFO as a mentor. Financialese is no different from any other jargon. There are basic concepts, and each of them has a name and/or an acronym. It's not enough to know what concepts are called; you must also understand them.

- Financial communications and investor relations are two different sides of a coin. If you opt for investor relations, you must not only know the language, but you also must be able to apply it to a specific industry or organization. Talking to financial analysts and shareholders is an art form of sorts. While you can learn many aspects of financial communications by the book, communicating with Wall Street requires a command of the facts, scrupulous honesty, and an understanding of industry trends.

Writers are perpetual students. We go to school all of our lives, learning about subjects that often seem to exist in a vacuum. What does railroad relocation have to do with music and art? How are construction, paperboard packaging, and mortgage financing related? You get the idea. If you are a generalist, as I have been, you go from one to another, sometimes feeling like a Mexican jumping bean. It takes years to see patterns, but believe me, they are there.

< 91 >

CHAPTER 20

BUSINESS COMMUNICATIONS

busi·ness (bîz´nîs) *noun*
1. a.) The occupation, work, or trade in which a person is engaged; b.) A specific occupation or pursuit: *the best designer in the business.*
2. Commercial, industrial, or professional dealings.
3. A commercial enterprise or establishment.
4. Often used to modify another noun: *a business computer; a business suit.*

com·mu·ni·ca·tions (ke-my¡˝nî-kâ´shens) *noun*
1. The exchange of thoughts, messages, or information, as by speech, signals, writing, or behavior.
2. A means of communicating, especially: a.) A system, such as mail, telephone, or television, for sending and receiving messages. b.) A network of routes for sending messages and transporting troops and supplies.
3. The technology employed in transmitting messages.

Business communications is what I have done for most of my career. Ideally, this segment of communications begins with determining what you want to say, to whom you want to say it, and how you're going to package the message. It's amazing how few clients are sure about any of those things. Many tend to begin at the end, which is the packaging. They

< 92 >

know they want to do direct mail or have an article written for a magazine or put together a PowerPoint presentation, but that is often as far as they have thought. The options are virtually without end and can seem quite daunting to a client. It's up to you to clarify and simplify them. Let's start with the message, which could be intended to do any of the following: announce a new presence in the market, enhance a corporate image, sell a product or service, manage a crisis, teach new skills, share news or information, explain a company policy, or communicate with the financial community.

Once the objective of the message is nailed down, you can move on to targeting a particular audience. How you ultimately frame the message depends very much on whom you're talking to and what that audience needs to know. Your client may want to communicate with one or more of these groups: customers or clients, employees, the public, shareholders and the financial community, a board of directors, industry peers or competitors, other businesses, or consumers. The language, style, and content of the message will vary from audience to audience. For example, it would probably have a promotional tone for customers; industry terms for peers or competitors; financial information for shareholders and analysts; and a more conversational, easy-to-understand style for employees.

When you know what you want to say and to whom, the last question is *how*? Should you advise your clients to announce the information in a meeting, plan an ad campaign, host a special event, do a direct-mail program, give a speech,

< 93 >

put out a newsletter, or produce a video. And those hardly cover all of the choices. Your client could also select from Internet or intranet websites, news releases, articles for trade and business magazines, annual reports, trade shows, training programs, or even a book. It will be up to you to know enough about the available media to facilitate an intelligent choice and, in many cases, write the material. (This is when you'll be grateful for becoming a generalist.)

How does all of this affect your role as a freelance writer? Is it possible to write knowledgeably about many industries and companies within those industries? Are you really expected to know what to say and how to say it to every audience? Should you be expected to be expert or even competent in all of these diverse media? If so, wouldn't you have to be a genius? The answer goes back to Chapter 16, "Telephoto or Wide-Angle Lens." Are you going to be all things to all clients or editors, or are you going to concentrate your efforts in a smaller circle of influence?

If it is the former, you will have to be a quick study when it comes to clients or assignments in various industries. While you will never learn everything you would want to know, you can keep building on what you have learned, especially if the client or publication hires you often. In terms of media, while some of us may try to do it all, there are some things we do better than others. I have expanded my repertoire of competencies over the years by just plunging in and flailing around. Often, that has worked, but when I knew I was in over my head, I have found an expert to help me or do it for me.

< 94 >

On the other hand, if you specialize in a particular kind of writing—ad copy, direct mail, speeches—you can apply these skills to any assignment. If you specialize in a specific industry—biochemistry, paper-based packaging, food and beverage—you can carve out a niche in those markets. In all cases, however, you should be familiar with the types of audiences you want to reach. With the help of your client or editor, you can learn to understand and write for each one.

In a sense, business communications is similar to marketing communications in that it has many subspecialties. You can dabble and thus improve in all of them or concentrate on one or more. The choice is yours, but it is always a good idea to do a bit of experimentation before you settle down and to be willing to venture out of your specialty when an opportunity presents itself.

< 95 >

CHAPTER 21

STYLE/GENRE

style (stīl) *noun*
1. The way in which something is said, done, expressed, or performed: *a style of speech and writing.*
2. The combination of distinctive features of literary or artistic expression, execution, or performance characterizing a particular person, group, school, or era.
3. A customary manner of presenting printed material, including usage, punctuation, spelling, typography, and arrangement.

gen·re (zhän´re) *noun*
A category of artistic composition, as in music or literature, marked by a distinctive style, form, or content: *"his six String Quartets . . . the most important works in the genre since Beethoven's"*

When I was in art school many years ago, most of my classmates wanted to be serious painters, as opposed to merely "commercial artists." The fact that making a living as a fine artist was uncertain at best forced many of them to reconsider and go into design or illustration instead. But when they opted out of growing up to be starving artists, I think they may have felt that they were selling out for the sake of financial security.

< 96 >

I have found the same thing to be true in the world of writing. So many writers I know seem to harbor a secret, or not so secret, desire to write fiction. Deep inside, they know, is a novel struggling to get out. Some day, when they have the luxury of time, they will write it. Or perhaps they are already working on it "on the side," just marking time until they can go off to a cabin in the woods and write in blessed solitude.

I confess I had one brief moment in my own life when the idea of writing a novel had great appeal. I had just begun to write and was trying a little bit of everything, from fillers for women's magazines to deep, thought-provoking essays. "Why not a novel?" I thought, and immediately plunged into a thinly disguised autobiographical fantasy.

My book had a carefully constructed plot, somewhat believable dialogue, and completely mixed-up geography, since I lived in St. Louis but set the story in New York and Chicago. There was one other thing wrong with it: It was a love story with a conspicuous lack of anything that resembled sex. My characters simply disappeared into a bedroom and emerged "after it was over," flushed and blissful. Chalk it up to youth and naiveté.

My novel was, if nothing else, cathartic and therapeutic. Whatever was "struggling to get out," apparently did, and, when it did, I had no need to continue. I knew how it was going to end, so there seemed to be no point in actually finishing it. I just put it in a box and went on to other things. It's still in that box, I imagine, and if I ever came across it in some cleaning frenzy, I'm not sure if I would even reread it.

< 97 >

While the subjects I tackle now are anything but light, my career actually began by writing tongue-in-cheek, humor pieces from my own experience. I wrote about our dog, who dropped out of (as in ran away) obedience training school; waiting until I was over forty to take up exercising; the impossibility of sustaining the Wonder Woman image in the real world; and dispelling the myth that business travel is glamorous and exciting. Humor was a catharsis, a way of dealing with the stuff of life. I left it for in-depth, heavily researched feature articles and often wondered how good I might have become if I had continued to develop that style.

More important than choosing a particular genre is *finding your voice*. By that I mean that each of us has a distinctive way of expressing ourselves—a rhythm or cadence to our sentences, an underlying philosophy that quietly permeates our work, even a way of using quotes and transitions to move a story along. For some people, writing style and speaking style are worlds apart, but for others they echo each other. Over the years, my unique voice has emerged and refined itself so that my writing has a distinctly recognizable quality to it. That makes it possible for me to write an annual report, a speech, a direct-mail piece, a video script, or a book, while still maintaining my own voice.

Some people write opinion pieces and essays; others dabble in short stories or poetry. Some specialize in features or scripts or hard news. Some try a little of everything. In my business, I found myself writing on subjects and in styles I would never have predicted. "What do you really want to write?" I am often asked.

< 98 >

After three decades of being a generalist, I knew the answer. I wanted to write books, especially books like this one. I was so fortunate to be able to pursue that dream, along with the kind of writing that paid the bills and put food on the table. The irony is that, as I write books for other people (ghostwrite), I find that I am still a generalist, at least in terms of subject matter. The subjects are as varied as they ever were, but instead of articles, corporate communications, and marketing materials, they are now much longer nonfiction books.

My advice to other writers is simply this: Figure out what you love, and find a way to do it. If it pays, great; if it doesn't, do it on the side. But you will never really reach your potential as a writer if you don't write.

< 99 >

CHAPTER 22

DIRECT MAIL

direct mail *noun* – **di·rect´-mail´** (dî-rèkt´mâl´, dì-)
adjective: Advertising circulars or other printed matter
sent directly through the mail to prospective customers
or contributors.

There is hardly a day when my little mailbox doesn't over-
flow with junk mail. While I find it very annoying, I still open
every piece, just in case. What may look like junk has occasionally turned out to be a bill or a check that would have
landed in the trash were it not for my compulsive vigilance.
But, aside from that little pause at my dining room table,
most of it goes from mailbox to the recycle bin in mere
minutes. When I think of all the trees that gave their lives to
produce that useless paper, my annoyance grows. What a
waste of resources, time, and money. Why does anyone
bother when they know it will never be read?

Well, for one thing, those who do bother genuinely expect
it to *be* read, or they wouldn't be having it designed, written,
printed, and mailed. Direct mail has a purpose, and that
purpose is to sell something. In my view much of the stuff
that ends up in my mailbox is either poorly done or is mailed
indiscriminately to an inadequate mailing list. But not all
direct mail is junk. In fact, much of it is very effective.

< 100 >

High-quality, effective direct mail is a blend of art and science. It is the result of a sound marketing strategy, the talents and expertise of people in a variety of disciplines, and a partnership between the project manager and the client. What distinguishes effective direct mail from trash? Several things: knowledge of the medium and the target market, a well-researched and coded list, good writing and design, and a method for assessing and evaluating the results. While the message may indeed drive the medium, writing is only one element of a well-crafted direct-mail program.

What is considered "good writing" for a magazine article, a brochure, or an annual report is not necessarily good writing for direct mail. Direct mail has to grab the attention of the recipient immediately and sufficiently to prompt that person to open and read it. Part of the lure, of course, is the design of the piece. Your words may be spectacular, but if no one is moved to read them, they are meaningless.

Unless you are the project manager, you may not be in a position to develop the concept, write the headlines and the copy, or tell the designer what you want the piece to look like. A more likely scenario is that you will be a member of a creative and technical team and may or may not have input into the message and how it is to be communicated. One of my clients is the president of a direct-mail firm, and it is he who works with the client, develops the concept, sketches out a rough layout, and writes the headlines. The writer and designer take it from there.

If you write good advertising or promotional copy, you will probably write good direct-mail copy, which often

< 101 >

includes clever, punchy headlines; concise, high-impact copy; and a clear message conveyed in a variety of ways. The more complex the message, the harder it is to get it across quickly and to hold the reader's attention. Sometimes, the copy determines the design; sometimes, you will be writing to fit the design. Ideally, you and the designer will work as a team.

If you have never written in direct mail and don't know where to begin, here are some ideas for testing the waters:

- **Read examples of direct mail.** Despite my earlier remarks about junk mail, some of what lands in my mailbox may be hidden jewels among the rocks. That's another reason I look at every piece. Occasionally I do find a gem—an eye-appealing envelope or folded card that entices me to open it.

- **Collect direct mail.** I tend to read the ones that are truly irresistible and tuck them in a file for future reference as an example of what works. Actually, it's not such a bad idea to save a few of the rocks as examples of what *doesn't* work. An interesting exercise is to analyze the effectiveness of several pieces and rewrite them in a way you think would have more pizzazz.

- **Read about direct mail.** Go to the library or bookstore and find books on the subject. There is a book for virtually every kind of writing you might ever want to explore, from screenplays to science fiction and from fiction to freelance writing. (You need look no further on that topic.)

< 102 >

- **Take a class or attend a workshop.** Writing classes can be fun, as well as educational, and you meet a lot of people who share your interest. While it's true that much writing is learned "by the seat of your pants," the more formal ways to learn can speed up the process considerably.

- **Learn on the job.** If you are lucky enough to have a mentor, ask that person to critique your attempts. You will get very honest feedback, and each criticism will contribute to your learning. If you get an assignment to write direct mail, and you have a natural affinity for the medium, go for it. This may seem risky, but sometimes your best work comes out of taking a risk and a fresh approach to a topic.

Direct mail is a specialty that takes some time to master, but then most specialties do take time. Few of us suddenly become experts in any of the many possible subjects or genres, but if you find that you are drawn to this one, by all means give it a try.

< 103 >

CHAPTER 23

TRAINING

Train, trained, train·ing, trains *verb, transitive*
1. To coach in or accustom to a mode of behavior or performance.
2. To make proficient with specialized instruction and practice.
3. To give or undergo a course of training: *trained daily for the marathon.*

My first encounter with the training industry was about twenty years ago when I went to work for a training and development firm. At that point, I knew nothing about training, and for a long time, it seemed quite mysterious to me. Within the company were two "gurus," one who wrote the programs and one who wrote the books. It was assumed that, since I was totally unqualified to do either, I would write *about* training in newsletters, brochures, advertising copy, direct mail, and articles. Since, up to that point in my career, I had been a magazine journalist, feature writer, and editor, all of this was as foreign to me as training. That is where my education in marketing communications really began.

Training, as I first experienced it, had two components: videos that embodied the basic principles of the program,

< 104 >

and seminars, at which these principles were taught, role played, and inculcated into the participants' behavior. It all seemed quite complicated at first. There were several programs, and I went through all of them, trying to sort out the common themes and fine distinctions. But it didn't take a brain surgeon to figure out that there really was only *one* program, taught from several different perspectives and at various levels of sophistication.

The more I immersed myself in the training industry, the more apparent it became that canned videos featuring talking heads and four-and-a-half-day seminars were being replaced by programs customized to clients' needs and a new technology called computer-based training, or CBT. The company I worked for stuck with canned videos and never ventured into CBT.

Training, I discovered, comes in an almost endless variety of forms, subject matter, and delivery. My employer dealt only with issues pertaining to interpersonal skills, but beyond that specialized area is a world of training in product knowledge, technology, customer service, computer programming, desktop publishing, software programs, and much, much more. And there seem to be almost as many ways to present the content as there are subjects.

One the ironies in my career was that, when I launched my own business, the first company I worked for was the American Management Association for which I wrote training programs in audio, script, and book form for years. I also had the opportunity to write video-based training for

< 105 >

my corporate clients—some, the same old talking heads; others, infinitely more creative, depending on the scope and budget of the client.

There are many ways to get into this field more intentionally than I did, though sometimes it is more fun to just dive in headfirst and learn as you go. That said, here are some fundamentals you should master before you write training programs.

- **Know your subject.** If it is one about which you have been writing for a long time, you have an advantage. If it isn't familiar, research it in every possible way. Interview the client and experts in the field; read the company's marketing materials if they exist; go to the library; surf the Web. You can't write about something that is completely foreign to you.

- **Know your form.** Will this training be delivered as a lecture; on video, audio, or interactive computer program; or on the Internet? Will it involve a workbook, seminar, long-distance learning, one-on-one consulting, or team activities? Will it be a one-day, one-week, or a multiple-session program? Will you have to create before-and-after tests, case studies, exercises, sidebars, charts and graphs, or interactive scenarios? Whatever the answers to each of these questions, if you don't know how to do it already, learn how. Each form has its own special techniques. Sometimes they overlap; sometimes they are unique to the genre.

< 106 >

- **Know your audience.** This is one of the fundamentals of writing. To whom are you speaking, and what is special about these people? What do they need from this training, and how can you most effectively provide it? Do they know the jargon and expect to see it in the materials? Is this beginning, intermediate, or advanced training? Are they likely to be receptive or resistant participants? Are there barriers you will have to break down in terms of language, approach, form, or content in order to facilitate learning?

How can you know all of these variables before you write? By finding out as much as possible on the front end. Query the client or editor. If possible, meet some of the participants. Study other similar training programs. Find out what has worked or not worked in the past and why. Put yourself in the place of the recipients of this information. Remember, you are creating something that is going to have an impact on real people, so don't let the writing get in the way of clear communication.

< 107 >

TECHNICAL WRITING

tech·ni·cal (tèk´nî-kel) *adjective*
1. Of, relating to, or derived from technique.
2. a.) Having special skills or practical knowledge
   especially in a mechanical or scientific field: *a
   technical adviser.* b.) Used in or peculiar to a
   specific field or profession; specialized: *technical
   terminology.*

writ (rît), **writ·ten** (rît´n) also **writ·ing, writes** *verb,
transitive*
1. To compose and set down, especially in literary or
   musical form: *write a poem; write a prelude.*
2. To express in writing; set down: *write one's thoughts.*
3. To communicate by correspondence: *wrote that she
   was planning to visit.*
4. To produce written material, such as articles or
   books.

As a generalist, to some degree, I write about a wide
variety of subjects in an equally wide variety of styles and
media. Even as I continue to expand my repertoire, though,
I must admit that I am simply better at some things than at
others. I know I write better conversational copy than
promotional copy, stronger feature articles than video

< 108 >

scripts, and almost anything better than financial subjects. In trying on all the labels associated with writing, one I never considered appropriate was "technical writer." Attending a meeting of a technical writers' group some years ago only confirmed that feeling. The people at the meeting all wrote proposals for engineering firms, software training manuals, or scientific materials. Their subject matter seemed worlds apart from the kind of writing I was doing, or so I thought.

I reassessed that position when I started my own business. My very first freelance assignment was writing a brochure for a high-tech manufacturing company, which was staffed almost entirely by physicists. I found myself approaching this completely foreign topic the same way I would approach any writing project. I listened, I asked a lot of questions, I fed back my understanding of what I had heard, and I requested clarification or rephrasing whenever it seemed necessary. The brochure was approved.

My second new client was a nationwide mortgage banking company. I knew nothing about mortgage banking and even less about getting approval for a home loan on a computer. The technology was so new and so confusing that even the people who were developing it didn't seem able to explain it coherently. Again, I asked endless questions until I understood the process well enough to write about it.

Looking back on the years before and since I became an independent writer, I realize that I have written about such topics as research and development, emergency-room medicine, law, science, heavy manufacturing, farm equipment, diseases and complex medical conditions, public utilities,

< 109 >

chemicals and pharmaceuticals, the petroleum industry, telecommunications, transportation, printing, and agriculture—all of which are technical. Of course, that had not occurred to me when I was writing about them. Apparently, whether I thought the label fit or not, I was and am a technical writer.

Labels are limiting. If I call myself a technical writer, does that mean I am not a feature writer, an author, or a speechwriter? Even as specialists, writing stretches us and expands our horizons beyond the boundaries we may have tried to establish. Whether we deliberately or accidentally wander into writing about technical subjects, how expert we become depends on many factors. Among them are our natural ability to grasp technical subject matter; our academic or professional background in a given subject; our facility for applying the principles of research and writing to any subject, regardless of its technicality; and our skill as writers.

Let's say you find yourself drawn to this genre. What would it take to begin and master it? Where would you begin, and what are some things you should consider?

- One place to begin is by starting out as an expert in some area of "technology." That designation covers a broad spectrum, which could include anything from engineering to medicine and science to computers. The point is to know your subject very well and then write about it. Knowledge and expertise are in great demand; if you are also a skilled writer, you have a great advantage.

< 110 >

• Another launching point is to choose a subject for which you have a real affinity, study it, begin to write about it, and continue to build on your knowledge. The more you know, the more your reputation as an expert will grow.

• Sometimes, a subject chooses you. It could be one assignment that leads to another or a client who invests time and money in your learning on the job. After a while, you find yourself knowing quite a bit about something you would never have pursued on your own.

The point is that, no matter how you and technical writing get together, you may be surprised at how much you enjoy it and how proficient you become. Whether you decide to make technical writing only one of the services you offer or zero in on it as your primary area of concentration, you will find it a valuable ability to have. In one sense, technical writing *is* a specialized area; in another, it is simply bringing all the same techniques and skills to concrete subjects that you would bring to any other writing project.

< 111 >

CHAPTER 25

PROFESSIONAL WRITING

pro·fes·sion·al (pre-fèsh´e-nel) *Abbr.* **prof.**
1. Of, relating to, engaged in, or suitable for a profession: *a professional field such as law; professional training.*
2. Engaging in a given activity as a source of livelihood or as a career: *amateur and professional actors.*
3. A person following a profession, especially a learned profession.
4. A skilled practitioner; an expert.

writ (rît) **writ·ing, writes** *verb, transitive*
1. To express in writing; set down: *write one's thoughts.*
2. To produce written material, such as articles or books.

Professional writing is an area traditionally associated with academics who must publish or perish. By "publish," it is assumed that the work will come out in a scholarly journal or a book meant for peers or students in the writer's field. Over the years, however, I have broadened my view of the kinds of writing that legitimately fit into this category.

For one thing, many professionals do write about their areas of expertise in vehicles other than academic journals

< 112 >

or textbooks. They may choose to write anything from training programs and self-help books to articles in jargon-free, conversational English. Just browse through any bookstore or library, and you will find hundreds of books on how to do virtually anything under the sun, written by experts in the fields of medicine, psychology, quantum physics, animal training, nutrition, addiction, child development, religion, finance, and scores of other disciplines.

These books sell. In fact, the self-help sections of most bookstores have continued to expand over the years, and *The New York Times Book Review* devotes a special section each week to the latest, not-to-be-missed self-help titles. Popular magazines for just about every audience are filled with scholarly articles bylined by writers with initials after their names. While some of these efforts are not very good, it's surprising how many are not only informative but also well written.

There are three ways freelance writers can reap the benefits of this genre. One is to be a professional in a particular field and write about it for a lay audience. Another is to specialize in a subject and build a reputation for writing authoritatively in that area. The third is to hook up with an expert who has a great deal to say but can't seem to say it without drowning the reader in technical terms or insider jargon. That person needs you, as an editor, a ghostwriter, or a co-author. The question is, how can you take advantage of these opportunities?

< 113 >

1. **A professional who writes in understandable, appealing language:** The best way to know a subject is to be in the field. If you are also fortunate enough to be able to communicate what you know in a way that non-experts can understand and enjoy, your opportunities are limited only by your imagination and marketing skills. Today's popular press is hooked on "how-to" articles, books, seminars, and presentations. Consider the best sellers on getting out of debt and investing, fixing troubled relationships, re-parenting your inner child, learning software programs (even if you are a "dummy"), finding the love of your life, meditating, managing people, motivating or disciplining employees, running a business, and on and on and on. You could quit your day job, and just write about what you know.

2. **A writer who specializes in a specific subject area:** The next best thing to being a bona fide expert by education or profession is to become one as a writer. Every subject I just mentioned is fair game for an enterprising writer who invests the time and effort to learn it well enough to write about it and keeps adding to that knowledge. As I mentioned in another chapter, gaining that knowledge may be a conscious choice or a matter of circumstances, but its origins don't really matter if you have an affinity for the subject.

< 114 >

3. An editor, ghostwriter, or a co-author for an expert: This one is the toughest route for most writers. It certainly has been for me. I've gone into several such projects thinking, Well, this person knows just everything about (fill in the blank). I'm an experienced interviewer. All I have to do is ask the right questions, draw him or her out, organize the material, translate it into English, and refine it. That's doable.

It may be doable, but it's tough. Such a project can fail in more ways than you can imagine, and I think I have experienced most of them. Here are just a few: The expert can't articulate what he knows; doesn't stick to the subject but wanders all over the place; is never satisfied with what you give him; wants it to sound more erudite or more folksy; demands to micro-manage every word; or can't believe you want to be paid, as opposed to doing this on the off chance that it may be a best seller.

I don't want to discourage you from this option, but neither do I want you to discover all the pitfalls the hard way—when you have committed to the project and are already knee-deep in frustration. On the other hand, sometimes you find a professional who knows her subject, can articulate it clearly, trusts your ability and judgment, and is willing to pay you for your time and effort. If that happens, my advice is, go for it. You may learn a lot, establish a valuable professional relationship, be paid what you deserve, and possibly even share the byline.

< 115 >

CHAPTER 26

BOOKS IN PRINT

book (b¢k) *noun*

1. A set of written, printed, or blank pages fastened along one side and encased between protective covers.
2. a.) A printed or written literary work. b.) A main division of a larger printed or written work: *a book of the Old Testament.*

print (prînt) *noun*

1. a.) Lettering or other impressions produced in ink from type by a printing press or other means. b.) Matter so produced; printed material. c.) Printed state or form.
2. a.) A printed publication, such as a book, magazine, or newspaper; b.) Printed matter.

Is it really every writer's dream to write a book? I've always thought so because it was *my* dream, but I've come to realize that there are probably as many dreams as there are writers. Mine came somewhat late. In fact, I was fifteen years into my career before it even crossed my mind. My first book was the result of doing a colleague a favor. He had committed to writing a series of "little books," as he called

< 116 >

them, but was too swamped to get them all done before the deadline. Could I help? Translation: Would I write three of them?

I panicked. I had never written a book. My writing style was much more journalistic than his. I would have to research all three subjects from scratch. I had a full-time job. The deadline was impossible. The editor didn't know a thing about me. It would be baptism by fire. And on and on and on. Of course, I said yes. The books were about professional image, resume writing, and conducting successful meetings. They really were *little*; each one was fifty pages long and could easily fit in a shirt pocket. I wrote one a month, made the deadline, and did not go up in flames.

Suddenly, I was an author, which looked nice on my resume but produced very little in the way of fame or fortune. I would have thought it was a fluke except that another editor called me and asked me to write a much-expanded version of one of the little books. When it was finished, it was notebook size and three hundred pages long. Having an editor at a reputable publishing company was like having the combination to a vault. One editor would introduce me to another, who would introduce me to someone else, who would keep that ball rolling. Most of the early assignments were how-to books, had tight deadlines, paid very little, and dealt with some aspect of getting along with people in a business setting. After a while, I was sure I had pretty well exhausted the subject of people skills.

When people learn that I am an author, they usually ask one of two questions: "Why don't you write a steamy romance

< 117 >

and make a lot of money?" or "When are you going to write the great American novel?" The answers are, "Because I don't want to," and "Never." I have no desire to read *or* write a steamy romance and never have. In fact, I don't even want to write fiction. It was difficult to explain to people how one could be in love with practical, business-oriented nonfiction. They just didn't get it.

After a while I expanded my horizons and eventually began to write about the most important topic in my life— writing—including this one on freelancing, another on how to write a nonfiction book, and a memoir on my then forty years as a writer.

"I'm thinking of writing a book," people often tell me. "But I just don't know where to start. What do I have to do?" Legend has it that, when some would-be sculptor asked Michelangelo how he created David, he is reported to have answered, "Well, I started with a large block of marble and chipped away everything that wasn't David."

Writing a book is not as mysterious as creating a David or a Pietá. Few of us are Michelangelos. We may never create a masterpiece, but we can write books. I have discovered that, when people ask me how to write a book, they want a short, sweet, all-inclusive answer that can be conveyed between two floors on an elevator. Here it is: *With a lot of planning, hard work, and tireless promotion.* Here is the longer answer. *There are six steps to writing, publishing, and promoting a nonfiction book. They include:*

< 118 >

1. **Planning** forces you to ask yourself many tough questions. It is much more than a mere exercise, because almost every word of it will eventually become a part of your book. If you have a conventional publisher, the plan will grow into a formal proposal, which will be required by the publisher or a literary agent.

2. **Writing** is the heart of the matter, the content, and the reason you are writing this book. You have either researched your subject or experienced it. You want to share it with others in a way that moves them, changes them, entertains them, or teaches them something. You want your readers not only to get your message but also to respond to it.

3. **Professional partners** are the people who will play a role in some aspect of your book, including everyone from editors to indexers and from proofreaders to publicists. The partners you choose depend on how elaborate your book will be, how you plan to publish, and how much money you have to spend.

4. **Production** is a series of activities between the completed manuscript and the published book. While you should be able to talk intelligently about this subject, you will not be expected to implement it. That is the job of a book designer who may be one of your professional partners or an expert provided by a conventional publisher.

< 119 >

5. **Publishing** is the step that enables people to read your book by converting files into print or electronic books. There are many more options for authors than there were years ago. Today, traditional publishing is only one of several options available to you. The more you know about those options, the better equipped you are to make the right choice.

6. **Promotion** lets your target audience know your book exists and how to buy it. The time to start thinking about promotion is not when your book is published; it is during the planning phase. The key to effective promotion in the twenty-first century is knowing how to capitalize on the power of the Internet.

One of the traits you need most to take a book from concept to completion is a long attention span. It takes a lot of time and concentration to conceive, write, publish, and promote a book. It is time consuming, labor intensive, excruciatingly detailed, and often frustrating; but, from my perspective, it is the most satisfying part of being a full-time freelance writer.

< 120 >

CHAPTER 27

ELECTRONIC PUBLISHING

e·lec·tron·ic (î-lèk-tròn´îk, ê´lèk-) *adjective*
1. Of or relating to the Internet.
2. Of or relating to electronics.

pub·lish (pùb´lîsh) *verb*
1. To prepare and issue (printed material) for public distribution or sale.
2. To bring to the public attention; announce. See synonyms for *announce*.
3. To be the writer or author of published works or a work.

Last year, after sending my proposal for a book on writing to the only four publishers who target this market—and striking out with all four—I was completely at a loss. I had an idea I was passionate about, a comprehensive proposal, a lot of time invested in research, but no agent or editor who was willing to take it on. I mentioned my quadruple rejection to one of my clients, who instantly responded, "Why don't you write an eBook and publish it online?"

I had no idea what an eBook was then. While eBooks were not yet a household word, they have long since entered the lexicon. There was much agreement in publishing and

< 121 >

high-tech circles that this was the way publishing was headed. Electronic publishers appeared on the scene, and software and eBook-reader manufacturers scrambled to develop the standard to which all electronically published materials would conform. One didn't have to be a futurist or clairvoyant to know this outcome was as inevitable as the emergence of the mouse, modems, and microchips.

Let me confess at the outset that I reinvented the wheel every step of the way and did things the hard way because I didn't yet know any other way. It was only when I attended a technology conference for independent writers that I began to understand the vast potential of this latest technological breakthrough. The keynote speaker for that conference was Pat Schroeder, a former member of Congress and an outspoken crusader for the protection of intellectual property. But she was only one of the many experts who covered every conceivable aspect of this "new wave" in publishing.

Electronic publishing was still on the horizon when *Going Solo* was first published in digital format (in 2002), but even then, it wasn't really an eBook. At the time, this new industry was struggling to be born, but there were problems. eBook readers and publishing software were confusing and expensive; there was no uniformity or ability to cross platforms; and no single competitor managed to capture the public's attention. So, after much fanfare, the whole effort fizzled out.

In 2007, Amazon introduced its first eBook reader—the Kindle—for $399. It took off like a rocket. Today, only six

< 122 >

years later, according to the Pew Research Center, one-fifth of all adults in this country have read at least one eBook, and 29 percent of Americans eighteen and older own one or more eBook reading devices. Sales of eBooks are growing at a faster rate than print books on Amazon. For authors, it is no longer a question of *whether* to publish electronically; it is *how* to do it most efficiently and cost effectively.

Let's say you have a completed manuscript for a book and are considering going the electronic route. Where do you begin? How do you keep from learning everything the hard way? If you Google eBook publishers, you will see at least fourteen on the first page. How do you know which one is best? And, finally, should you do it yourself, publish to an eBook store, or use an eBook aggregator?

1. If you decide to **do it yourself**, check out *Publish Your Own Ebooks: How To Write, Publish & Sell Ebooks Online* by Gary McLaren, who also publishes Worldwide Freelance on the Web. It is a step-by-step guidebook on everything you need to know to self-publish.

2. **eBook stores** publish and sell eBooks. Browse Amazon's Kindle Store, Barnes & Noble eBooks, Sony Reader Store, Taylor & Francis eBookstore, Cambridge eBookstore, BooksOnBoard, Random House eBooks, and Powell's Books eBooks. Read the websites and read comparisons on other sites before you decide.

< 123 >

3. **eBook aggregators** are liaisons between eBook authors and eBook retailers, such as Apple and Sony. Some aggregators offer design, formatting, and distribution. Here are a few of the top ones: Smashwords, FastPencil, BookBaby, Baker & Taylor, Copia, and EbookIt. (Just for the record, I use BookBaby.)

Just remember, an eBook should meet all the same high standards as a printed book. It should be well written, edited and copy edited, formatted to meet the requirements of the eBook store or aggregator, and have a well-designed cover. Your reputation as a writer and an author are riding on the level of quality of all aspects of your eBook.

< 124 >

CHAPTER 28

WRITING FOR THE WEB

In·ter·net (în´ter-nèt˝) *noun*
Computer science.
A matrix of networks that connects computers around
the world.

World Wide Web *noun*
Computer science.
An information server on the Internet composed of
interconnected sites and files, accessible with a browser.

Writing for the Internet is a whole new ball game. For one
thing, the less you write, the better it is. No one wants to
wreck his eyesight poring over a screen full of words. For
another, the words that are there really have to say something and say it fast. There is a new breed of "readers" out
there in cyberspace, and they seem to have one thing in
common—a short attention span. It's a fickle crowd. If
something is boring, self-serving, or slow to download, with
a click of a mouse, they are off to something else.

More important than words (isn't this always the case?)
are the graphics. Graphics attract. If they do their job well,
some Web surfer, somewhere in the world, may actually
read what you write. And then there are a million bells and

< 125 >

whistles to draw attention to your words. They can slide onto the page, flash on and off, appear from nowhere, change shape and color before your eyes, and lead the viewer quickly and deftly to the next screen. What you write and how Web designers get people to read it are as much art as science.

Nothing prepares you for your first assignment, or at least nothing prepared me. "Can you write for the Web?" a new client asked me. "Of course," I said, assured that if I could write, I could write for the Web. Not so, it seems. "Let's start with the flash piece," he suggested. Not knowing what a flash piece was, I wrote too much. That project, I'm sorry to say, didn't go well, but it did teach me this sad truth: If one can write, it doesn't necessarily mean she can write for the Web. It's a bit more complicated than that.

Let's say you do all the writing for one of your clients, and that client—who is being pulled kicking and screaming into the 21st century—finally concedes that the company does need a website. How do you avoid the potential pitfalls and deliver a website that does the job? Here are some of the things I have learned since my first unsuccessful assignment.

The Basics

- **Get down to some serious surfing.** Visit all kinds of websites but particularly those in the same industry. How are competitors telling their stories? What are they saying? What are they showing? How are they grabbing attention and then keeping it? If you're intrigued, study the site to

< 126 >

see what is working. If you are totally bored, study the site to see why your fingers are itching to move on.

- **Review the materials you have already written for this client.** What is the story the client has been telling by way of print or electronic media? What are the salient points that must be included in the website copy? How can you adapt those points for this particular medium?

- **Don't go it alone unless you are also a crackerjack Web designer.** There are too many ways to make mistakes even if you know what you are doing, which, chances are, you don't. Team up with an expert who knows the design and technical sides of the business. Then put your heads together to conceive and create the best possible product. This is quite different from writing to fit an existing design or handing over the copy and hoping it will fit.

- **Write to inform as well as to sell.** People can spot a self-serving site that screams LOOK AT ME in neon. If you have a product, show them what it is and what it can do. If you offer a service, especially a complex one, let the designer make it easier to understand. The Web's purpose is to share information. Whatever path, or search engine, people use to get to your site, be assured they won't stay long if there is nothing in it for them.

- **Vary the content.** You want Google and other search engines to find you; you want prospects and customers to

< 127 >

visit more than once. But if they come back and nothing has changed, they probably won't make a return visit. You have to make it worth their while to click that mouse.

Beyond the Basics

Once upon a time, this would have been all you needed to know to write for the Web, but because this medium has changed faster than most of us can even hope to grasp, let alone keep up with, it's a whole new ball game. That was back in the days of Web 1.0, though no one called it that at the time. What has changed, besides technology, is the focus. Here is where we've been, where we are, and where we are going:

- **Web 1.0** – In the olden days of the Internet, websites dispensed information, and people were limited to merely viewing content. Like advertising, it was one-way communication. Websites were characterized by read-only content and static HTML. We were all passive recipients of the message.

- **Web 2.0** – Along came Web 2.0, which is about *consuming* as well as *contributing* information through blogs or websites, blurring the lines between the consumer and publishers of content publishers. Web 2.0 was all about interaction, collaboration, conversation, and relationships. Now we don't only receive the message; we also respond to it.

< 128 >

- **Web 3.0** – On the horizon is something called the Semantic Web, which is all about personalization, intelligent search, and behavioral advertising, among other things. According to the World Wide Web Consortium (W3C)—an international community that develops open standards to ensure the long-term growth of the Web—"The Semantic Web provides a common framework that allows data to be shared and reused across application, enterprise, and community boundaries."

Yes, this may be a new medium for you. Yes, it is changing all the time. Yes, there is a steep learning curve. But hasn't that been true of everything you have ever tackled? Hasn't it all been new and different? Haven't you been learning every day of your career, and won't you continue to learn forever? Of course. This is the direction in which the world is moving, and, just as you always have, you will move with it.

< 129 >

CHAPTER 29

MULTIMEDIA

mul·ti·me·di·a (mùl´tê-mê´dê-e, -tì-) *plural noun (used with a sing. verb)*
1. The combined use of several media, such as movies, slides, music, and lighting, especially for the purpose of education or entertainment.
2. The use of several mass media, such as television, radio, and print, especially for the purpose of advertising or publicity. Also called *mixed media.*
3. The combined use of media such as text, graphics, video, and sound, as on a computer system. *noun, attributive:* Often used to modify another noun: a multimedia presentation; *a multimedia advertising campaign.*

Multimedia used to require an overhead or 35mm projector, which was soon supplanted by behind-the-scenes, multiple slide projectors, complete with sound and special effects. Then, presenters had to become proficient in Power-Point or some other presentation-graphics program in order to produce full-scale, computer-generated presentations with bells and whistles and projection capabilities. Then, of course, those slides had to be projected from a laptop computer onto a huge screen. But, like everything in the

< 130 >

world of information technology, what was once state of the art is now considered primitive.

Multimedia, today, is far more than computerized slide presentations. It includes video, graphics, sound effects, animation, music, website production, and all of the sophisticated software that makes all of these components work. The good news is, that no matter how graphic dependent multimedia may be, words continue to be the foundation upon which communication is built. From development to presentation, words are the vehicles that give shape and purpose to all forms of multimedia. The opportunities to write and sell in this arena can only expand. On the other hand, the competition is going to expand just as fast, and writers must not only learn to function in this visual world but to take risks and become innovators.

Writing is essentially a linear process, no matter how creative it may be. "Linear" suggests that the left side of one's brain dominates the process of writing. Graphics, movement, and spatial concepts tend to be right-brain activities. This requires a whole different way of processing information. If this is new to you, where do you begin? Of course, you can surf the Web, read books, and view successfully executed projects, which tend to be my first approach to new things. But another way to learn is by simply taking the plunge and experimenting by doing, even if you have no idea what you're doing.

In another lifetime, I turned to books to learn a new subject; now, I "Google" it—a habit that required much reprogramming of the gray matter in my brain.

< 131 >

One of the most difficult adjustments for a writer working in this new arena is letting go of many of the ideas associated with putting words on paper. I have found this particularly difficult. I print out my e-mail, think print instead of screen when I'm working on an eBook, and am constantly surprised when the words on my website aren't as readable as I had envisioned. Multimedia encompasses all of the senses simultaneously. For a writer, to think about movement, sound, and visual images requires new and expanded ways of recognizing the many ways in which information can be communicated.

If there is a bottom line here, in my view, it is this: Change is inevitable, constant, and rapid. Nowhere is that more apparent than in the field of communication. Writers have always faced this reality and met its challenge. Just as we have progressed from quill pens and parchment to keyboards, colored monitors, and voice-activated word processing, we are now well into the next phase and still learning. Inherent in being a writer is being a lifelong student, no matter how scary the new lessons may seem.

I learned this lesson through negative and positive examples. The former was the end of a career of a CFO who could not abandon manual record keeping for computerized accounting and was displaced by someone who wasn't afraid to learn. The latter was the success of an author in his sixties, who had written on yellow legal pads all his life, yet learned to type and then to compose on a computer. One either learns and grows or becomes a dinosaur. The choice seems obvious to me.

< 132 >

CHAPTER 30

FEATURE ARTICLES

fea·ture (fê´cher) *noun*
A prominent or special article, story, or department in a newspaper or periodical.

ar·ti·cle (är´tî-kel) *noun*
A nonfictional literary composition that forms an independent part of a publication, as of a newspaper or magazine.

I spent the first half of my career writing feature articles and thought for years that no other genre could be half as satisfying. When I began, I had no idea what a feature article was, what its characteristics might be, or how to write one. Actually, I sort of stumbled into this form and, only after *much* on-the-job training, managed to develop my own voice.

At first, my articles were first-person humor pieces about whatever was going on in my life at the moment. They included such topics as our collie, the dog school drop out; my addiction to cleaning ladies; the dubious joys of business travel; and, my favorite, the perils of physical fitness over forty. In the midst of trying to perfect my tongue-in-cheek style, I landed a real assignment that required stepping out of first person and into third.

< 133 >

My approach was purely intuitive. Somehow, I seemed to *know* how to use narrative to string quotes together, how to attribute quotes so that they sounded immediate rather than in past tense, and how to capture and convey an interviewee's enthusiasm for the subject. That does not mean that these early efforts were particularly good, only that I apparently had a natural affinity for feature writing. Obviously, a writer can't go on indefinitely by winging it and hoping for the best. This writer had a lot to learn and many opportunities to do so. I freelanced for four-and-a-half years before my meteoric rise (really!) from ad space salesperson to magazine editor. Every job I ever had was based on my ability to write and edit features.

In the early eighties, I put together a writers workshop on feature writing and almost immediately discovered that I would have to analyze what I was doing if I planned to teach it. The analysis revealed that every article was the result of a foolproof process that never varied. The question was, could I teach that process? The answer turned out to be 95 percent "yes." The process was simply a logical sequence of steps, and the promise I made to my students was this: If you follow this process—in order—by the end of the eighth session, you will be putting an article that is as good as we can possibly make it into an envelope and sending it to an editor who has agreed to read it. One hundred percent of those who followed those steps were published. The process had eight steps:

< 134 >

1. Choose a topic. Start with an idea. Is there something you have a burning desire to write about or a particular publication you want to write for? If you are connected with such a publication, the topic may be an assignment. Perhaps you are in public relations and the client has defined the subject matter for you. Of course, there are many times when you have no idea what to write about and will have to create your topic out of whole cloth.

Once you have decided what to write about, the next step is to establish your premise. What is the point of your article, your working theme? You should be able to sum it up in a sentence or two. For example, when I was hired by four St. Louis law firms to write about the growing importance of law firm marketing, my working hypothesis was, in order to compete in an increasingly complex, changing environment, many law firms across the country were exploring a revolutionary new strategy—marketing their services.

2. Research. Research has three purposes: (1) It either reaffirms and expands your hypothesis, or it reveals that you are on the wrong track and need to start over. (2) In its early stages, research provides enough information to help you block out the article and write a coherent, convincing query letter. (3) Finally, it fills in the meat of your article. Information is gathered through interviews, reading, and, increasingly, making expert use of the resources on the Web. No writer can survive today without being Internet savvy.

< 135 >

3. Draft a query letter. Unless you are on assignment, the idea is to sell your article to an editor, and a good query letter is key to making that sale. A query letter parallels a sales call. It should have five parts, and, ideally, each should be only one paragraph long. (Editors are bleary-eyed from the amount of reading material that lands in their in-boxes.)

a. The first paragraph is your introduction. It tells the editor who you are, why you're writing, and the subject of your proposed article.

b. The second paragraph focuses on the editor's needs, and to write it you must know the general editorial policy of the publication and the audience to whom it is directed. The editor wants to know two things: Do you understand what he or she needs, and how is your article going to fill that need?

c. The third paragraph briefly describes the content and appropriateness of your article and why the publication's readers would want this information.

d. The fourth paragraph explains why you are uniquely qualified to write this piece. What are your credentials? How much do you know about this subject? How well do you understand the aims of the publication?

e. The final paragraph is very short. It is your close, your action statement, in which you state what you will do next. Will you wait to hear from the editor (risky), or will you call to follow up and, if so, when? If you say you'll call at a certain time, do so.

< 136 >

Use your follow-up call to ask questions. Ask what the editor looking for. Is there a particular point of view or style he prefers? What should you avoid? How can you best meet the needs of the readers? If you don't know what those needs are, you are more likely to miss them than to meet them. So, do your homework, i.e., read several issues of the publication before you write this letter.

4. **Do more research.** Don't sit around waiting for a response. Go back to researching, this time in much more depth. Immerse yourself in your subject. Gather every bit of information you can find from every available source. (In the first incarnation of *Going Solo*, Google was not yet a search-engine giant or a verb.) Talk to as many experts or sources as possible. Keep at it until you are filled to the point of overflowing. When you feel that one more fact will be a fact too many, you'll know it's time to stop.

5. **"Feed the computer."** I named this step in my process years before I ever saw a computer and have never been able to find a better way to describe it. This is the time to input all the data you have gathered into the computer that is *your own mind.* For many writers, this is the toughest step of all and one they often just skip. I never skip it because I think it is critical. It can take anywhere from a couple of hours to the better part of a day, and it entails sitting down and reading, highlighting, making notes, and organizing every piece of information you have

< 137 >

gathered. What's so hard about that? Other than the time and concentration it requires, not too much. But what *is* hard is walking away and putting it out of your mind. Read a book, play golf, go to a movie, go to sleep, but drop it from you conscious thoughts. You've put the data in; the "computer" will do the rest. Believe me, it works!

6. **Write.** This is what all that preparation has been leading to—the moment when everything comes together into a coherent whole. If you've followed the first five steps, you will find that you're more than ready to write. Obviously the intricacies of how to do it would require a separate book. The most difficult thing for most new writers is learning how to incorporate quotes into an article so that they sound plausible and natural. The quotes should tell the story, make the points, and move the story along. The narrative, on the other hand, holds it all together and ties one point to another.

7. **Revise and edit.** There are two approaches to writing: One is to start writing, keep going until you're finished, and fix it later. The other is to write a paragraph or even a sentence and polish it until it seems perfect. I think it's a matter of personal style, but whichever you choose, eventually, you will have to reread, revise, and edit. Your first draft is just that—a first draft. Even if it's a great first draft, it will have to be refined before it is truly complete.

< 138 >

Editing is not a mysterious or highly technical process. It simply means that you read your article very carefully, looking for typos, grammatical errors, repetitive words, and awkward phrasing. I have always found it useful to read my articles aloud because I tend to hear things I miss when I read. Editing provides the opportunity to see the big picture, as well as the details; to fix the glitches; and to polish the prose. As with researching and writing, there is an optimal moment to stop. When one more change might just topple your carefully constructed story, it's time to print it one last time and turn off the computer.

8. **Send your manuscript to an editor.** Step 8 is the payoff. After your query letter and follow-up calls, the best-case scenario is when an editor says, "That sounds interesting. I'd like to take a look at it when it's finished." There is no sweeter moment—except perhaps, seeing it in print—than dropping that envelope in a mailbox when you know someone is waiting for it.

< 139 >

CHAPTER 31

WRITING FOR WRITERS

writ·ing (rĭˊtĭng) *noun*
1. The act of one who writes.
2. Written form: *Put it in writing.*
3. The occupation or style of a writer.

writ·er (rĭˊter) *noun*
One who writes, especially as an occupation.

Writing for writers is big business, one I seem to be supporting single-handedly. I have shelves of books for and about writers, not to mention the classic references by Webster, Bartlett, Roget, and Strunk and White. And, if any of them fail me, I can always turn to Google on my computer or a least a half-dozen grammar sites on the Web. Beyond books, there are writers' magazines, writers' lists and chat rooms, e-zines, eBooks, electronic and print-on-demand (POD) publishers, and software programs for writers.

It makes sense for writers to write about what we know best, whether that is how to write a screenplay, a romance novel, a feature article, or literary criticism. I wanted to write about what it takes to make it as a freelance writer, because I *am* a freelance writer and because I felt I had a great deal to share. Before one writes a book, of course, it's a good idea to see what else is out there on the same subject.

< 140 >

My research revealed fifty-three books on freelance writing. (That was in 2002. A quick trip to Amazon just now revealed *2,496* books.) In analyzing the titles, I found that they naturally fell into three categories: general books on freelance writing; freelancing as a business; and areas of specialization, such as greeting cards, magazine features, straight news, technical writing, copywriting, corporate communications, and writing for the BBC.

When I say analyze, I mean *analyze.* I crawled around the floors of bookstores. I went to the library. I searched Amazon and Barnes & Noble. I read book jackets and book reviews. In some cases, I read entire books, not to mention buying them to add to my own library. It was both intimidating and enlightening. What could I possibly have to say that had not already been said and said authoritatively and articulately? What could I add to this mix, and what made me think anyone would want to read it? I think these are questions every writer must ask before embarking on a book for other writers. Do you understand the art of writing in a particular genre better than anyone else? Do you really have anything new to say about English grammar? Is your approach to the writing life all that unusual or inspirational? Are you adding anything new to the existing body of work?

Well, yes, was my answer to that last question. What I wanted to tell aspiring and working freelancers *was* unique to my experience and perspective, and the way I wanted to present it was unlike anything else I had seen. I couldn't find a single book written by an authority on this subject that was both memoir and a how-to. And there

< 141 >

seemed to be dearth of good books on freelance writing in the eBook titles I found.

There are other questions a would-be author must answer. A good way to find out what they are is to read a very good book on how to write a book proposal. My favorite is *Nonfiction Book Proposals Anybody Can Write* by Elizabeth Lyon. By the time you finish researching the answers, you will know whether or not to write your book. I decided to write mine. There is another very important factor in this decision: obsession. Frankly, I was and am obsessed with this project. I wanted to write it because I *had to write it.* I didn't seem to have a choice; it demanded to be written.

Not only did I want to write it, I wanted to teach it. I wanted, then and now, to help writers write. This obsession has grown stronger over the years. The original *Going Solo* was followed by seven editions of *How to Write a Nonfiction Book: From planning to promotion in 6 simple steps, Words To Live By: Reflections on the writing life from a 40-year veteran,* several years in a classroom teaching aspiring authors how to write a book, and an online course on the same subject.

The point of all of this is: if you know your particular genre or area of specialization well enough to want to share it with others (for profit, as well as love), take that possibility seriously. Do your homework; keep in touch with your growing desire to do it; and, if all the indications point in that direction, go for it! (Please keep in mind that this advice is coming from a zealot.)

< 142 >

SECTION III

_____

BALANCING ACT:

*How to play all the roles
of a freelance writer*

< 143 >

CHAPTER 32

DOING WHAT YOU LOVE, LOVING WHAT YOU DO

love, loved, lov·ing, loves *verb, transitive*
1. To have a deep, tender, ineffable feeling of affection and solicitude.
2. To have a feeling of intense desire and attraction toward someone or something.
3. To like or desire enthusiastically: *loves swimming.*
4. To thrive on; need: *The cactus loves hot, dry air.*

work (wûrk) *noun*
1. Physical or mental effort or activity directed toward the production or accomplishment of something. a.) A job; employment. b.) A trade, profession, or other means of livelihood.
2. Something that one is doing, making, or performing, especially as an occupation or undertaking; a duty or task: An amount of such activity.
3. Something that has been produced or accomplished through the effort, activity, or agency of a person or thing: *This story is the work of an active imagination.*
4. An artistic creation, such as a painting, sculpture, or literary or musical composition; a work of art.

< 145 >

It is every writer's dream—in fact, it is every *person's* dream—to earn a living doing the work he or she truly loves. Bookstore shelves are full of self-help titles designed to help people figure out what they want to do and how to do it. Sadly, many people are either so completely out of touch with their inner desires that they have no idea of what they want to do, or they are so overwhelmed with the vast array of career possibilities open to them that they become immobilized. Although there are many people out there who have not yet discovered their calling, for the most part, writers are not plagued with this problem. Most of us know without a doubt that we want to be writing; the challenge is to figure out how to support ourselves doing it.

As I taught writing over the years, I encountered students who had knock-your-socks-off talent but no drive or follow through, and others with minimal talent but an insatiable desire to write. At first, I was surprised at who did well and who did not; but after a while, I could accurately predict. Obsession and sheer will had a stunning power that overcame any deficiencies in inborn ability, whereas talent alone was never quite enough.

Of course, there are some bona fide geniuses out there who are so good at what they *do*; whatever they *don't* do is overlooked. But these people are rarely on their own, juggling clients and editors, deadlines and details, business and marketing plans, billing and collecting money, and the myriad minutia freelancers must do in order to survive. I know this is a rash generalization; but in my experience, geniuses tend to be writing novels or poetry or memorable

< 146 >

advertising slogans, like "Things go better with Coke," "You've come a long way, baby," or "This Bud's for you." There are also writers who get to do what they love, but in circumstances they hate, and those who have jobs they love in every respect except that they don't involve writing in any meaningful way. If you fall into either of these categories, you are either contemplating freelancing or already doing it. So, what's the problem? The problem, unless you have a trust fund, is making enough money to support yourself, at the very least, and to live a quality life, at most. (Personally, I'd prefer the latter.) If you really want to love what you do and do what you love, here are four ways to go about it:

- **Find a writing job in an environment that fosters autonomy and creativity.** If you want to be assured of a steady paycheck for doing what you want to do, this is certainly your best option. Other than putting up with all that goes with working for someone else, this approach provides a number of pluses: financial security, professional stability, people to talk to, feedback and creative input from others, and structure. That's the good news; the bad news is that such jobs are pretty hard to find. Landing a writing job is a challenge in itself, but it is nothing compared to finding one in an organization that allows you space and autonomy.

- **Find a good-paying, full-time job you enjoy, and free- lance part time on the side.** If a dependable source of

< 147 >

income is one of your non-negotiable criteria, and option #1 doesn't pan out, another approach is to keep your full-time vocation and your part-time avocation separate. As long as you can maintain enough psychic and physical energy to write, it is possible to carve out time to freelance as well. That may be all you need; but if it isn't, consider the next option.

- **Begin now to build a freelance business that eventually will become full time.** Novice swimmers don't compete at the Olympic level without intense preparation. They train, they practice, they build their form and self-confidence over time, and they work their way up the competitive ladder. Only when they are sure they're ready, do they compete at the highest level. Part-time writing is the best kind of training because it gives you the same opportunity to practice—to polish your skills, build your confidence, and learn the ropes—*before* you go for the gold.

- **Build a financial safety net, do the groundwork, and take the plunge.** No matter which way you approach full-time freelance writing, remember that it is a *business*, as well as a creative venture. It takes a lot of planning to start a business, and one of the most important aspects of that planning is being sure you can support yourself for six months to a year, even if you don't earn a penny. Doing the groundwork means learning everything else you need to do, from printing business cards to keeping accurate

< 148 >

financial records, from building a database of potential clients or editors to showing your portfolio, and from writing an informal contract to enforcing its terms when the work is completed. There is an optimum moment to hang out your shingle, and you will know when you're ready to take that step. Just trust your instincts.

Henry David Thoreau observed that "The mass of men lead lives of quiet desperation." For writers, such a life is one in which they do not write. I believe that doing what you love and loving what you do is not only a possibility but also a human being's prerogative.

< 149 >

CHAPTER 33

WRITING ON THE SIDE

write (rìt) *verb*
wrote (rot) **writ·ten** (rît´n) **also writ** (rît) **writ·ing,
writes**
1. To form (letters, words, or symbols) on a surface such as paper with an instrument such as a pen.
2. To compose and set down, especially in literary or musical form: *write a poem; write a prelude.*
3. To express in writing: *write one's thoughts.*
4. To produce written material, such as articles or books.

side (sìd) *noun*
1. In addition to the main part; supplementary: *a side benefit.*
2. a.) One of two or more opposing individuals, groups, teams, or sets of opinions. b.) One of the positions maintained in a dispute or debate.
3. Minor; incidental: *a side interest.*

There is a certain romance associated with freelance writing. What is *not* romantic (in real life) is the idea of living on the street or being unable to go to the grocery store and the gas station in the same week. Making a living as an independent writer can be done; but for most of us, it's a long,

< 150 >

tough road. Perhaps that's why so many people give up on their dreams before they even reach the level of consciousness. I know I did. For years, I refused to let my dream of being a full-time, self-employed writer surface because it seemed so utterly impossible. I was, after all, gainfully employed in a writing job, which was more than many people could say. Shouldn't that have been enough?

My career began as a freelancer, and in some respects, that aspect of my life never skipped a beat. My first full-time job after doing the stay-at-home-mom thing was with a local newspaper. I wanted to write; they wanted me to sell advertising space. We made a deal: I would sell space full time if they would let me freelance for them part time. They agreed. Only when I was editing a city magazine did I devote all of my writing time to one job. Actually, I devoted all of my *life* to that job. But ever after, no matter what I did from nine to five or eight to six or all kinds of crazy hours, I continued to write what I wanted to write on my own time.

I was employed as a writer or editor or both for twenty years. For much of that time my jobs were demanding and exhausting. Everything grew—responsibility, hours, stress, even salary; yet, I never made much money until my very last job. That was one reason I continued to write on the side, but even with a fairly well-paying job, the lure was irresistible. I had visions of writing for a national magazine. Then, one day, out of the blue, the phone rang; and a voice said, "I am the editor of *Sky* (Delta Airlines' in-flight magazine), and you have been referred to me by one of our photographers." I almost fell off my chair. The photographer had been a

< 151 >

nineteen-year-old novice when I first hired him. Ten years later, he was a very successful professional who remembered me.

The assignment was to write an article for *Sky's* series on CEOs around the country. The CEO in question was almost a legend in both local and national corporate circles. I don't think I had ever done so much advance research or been so prepared for any interview. When I walked into that man's office, wearing my best suit and carrying a tape recorder, I probably knew more about him than anyone except his wife. He was charming, articulate, and candid; I was mesmerized. As I asked questions and he answered them, I had a momentary glimpse into the future. I knew without a doubt that I was seeing my career as it would be someday.

Part-time freelancing was no longer enough. After six-and-a-half years with the same company, I was burned out on company politics, musical job descriptions, and tyrannical managers. It was time to give the dream a chance—full time. If it didn't work, I told myself, I could always get another job. As it turned out, I never did.

< 152 >

CHAPTER 34

LOVE/HATE RELATIONSHIPS

love (lùv) *noun*
A deep, tender, ineffable feeling of affection and solicitude toward a person, such as that arising from kinship, recognition of attractive qualities, or a sense of underlying oneness.

hate (hât) *verb*
hat·ed, hat·ing, hates *verb, transitive*
1. a.) To feel hostility or animosity toward. b.) To detest.
2. To feel dislike or distaste for: *hates washing dishes.*

re·la·tion·ship (rî-lâ´shen-shîp˝) *noun*
1. The condition or fact of being related; connection or association.
2. A particular type of connection existing between people related to or having dealings with each other.

Being a freelance writer is all about relationships—relationships with editors, agents, clients, designers, photographers, printers, computer experts, interview sources, and other writers. It's an understatement to say that such a career requires well-honed people skills and that developing and sustaining relationships are essential to success. When I was first planning this chapter, I thought I would call it "Clients

< 153 >

You Love, Clients You Hate," since most of my current work is with clients. That, of course, completely ignores the many writers who are sustained by editors rather than clients.

"Love/Hate Relationships" not only covers both scenarios, it also captures the ambiguous nature of our feelings towards those who pay our "salaries." I hope you have encountered at least one or two clients or editors who fall into the too-good-to-be-true category. When you do, you probably pinch yourself, simply because they are such a rare breed. These are the people who return phone calls, respond to query or marketing letters, respect your work, pay you what you're worth (on time), and try not to make unreasonable demands. They are all candidates for sainthood, in my opinion.

At the other extreme are those who are rude, arrogant, disrespectful, demanding, unrealistic, over-controlling, and penny pinching. Working for them is stress squared because they leave you feeling diminished and drained. On the bright side, as a freelancer, you do not have to do business with people like that. You can turn down the job at the outset; address the problems when they surface; and, if you choose to, resign from the project. My feeling is that, no matter how much you think you need the money, nobody needs it that much.

When I was a full-time employee, I can't even count the number of times I bit my tongue, compromised a principle, or tolerated unacceptable behavior from a boss—because, I told myself, I didn't want to risk my livelihood. Jobs like mine were not that easy to come by ... I had two children to support ... I would never live down the humiliation ... and

< 154 >

on and on and on. Getting fired was the worst possible thing I could imagine; and then, one day, the worst possible thing happened.

Amazingly, I did not die; my children did not starve or become homeless; I did get over it; and I felt free for the first time in my career. The worst possible thing turned out to be the best possible thing. One of the reasons was knowing that I would *never* again remain in an abusive situation. I knew there would always be another assignment, another client, or another job, just around the corner. In the last twenty-five years, I have had to test my resolve on more than one occasion, though, fortunately, not many. I have walked out of a meeting. I have confronted a client who was way out of line. I have stated, unequivocally, that I found the person's behavior unacceptable and, if it didn't stop, I would leave immediately. It stopped. I have not accepted lucrative jobs when the red flags were too numerous to ignore. I have even cancelled contracts when the situations became unbearable.

These, of course, are worse-case scenarios, but they illustrate the underside of freelancing. Not everyone you encounter will be professional or even civil. Some people are very difficult, if not impossible, to work with (See *Solving People Problems* (Amacom) for an entire book on this subject). But nowhere is it written that you have to grin and bear it. You don't.

In between these two extremes are the people you are more likely to work with or for. They are neither saints nor villains; they are just regular folks. They run the gamut of quirks and personalities, good days and bad, consistency

< 155 >

and professionalism. For the most part, you won't love them or hate them. You may develop relationships with them, or you may never get past being seen as a "vendor." You may admire some things about them and dislike others. And you may even put up with less-than-optimum working conditions from time to time. But that is the reality of the world of work and certainly of freelance work.

Years ago, when I was working for a large corporation and having a particularly bad day, I was crying the blues to my printing salesman. Finally, he shrugged and said, "Well, Bobbi, that's why they call it work and not sandbox." I've often thought of having that put on a banner and hanging it over my desk.

< 156 >

CHAPTER 35

FINDING WORK

find (fīnd) *verb*
found (found) find·ing, finds *verb, transitive*
1. To come upon, often by accident; meet with.
2. To come upon after a search: *found the hidden leak in the pipe.*
3. To obtain or acquire by effort: *found the money by economizing.*

work (wûrk) *noun*
1. Physical or mental effort or activity directed toward the production or accomplishment of something.
2. a.) A job; employment: *looking for work.* b.) A trade, profession, or other means of livelihood.
3. Something that one is doing, making, or performing, especially as an occupation or undertaking.

Work is the central issue of a freelance writer's life—the ability to find work and the desire and ability to do it. When I first began freelancing, close to forty-five years ago, finding the work wasn't much of a problem. I wrote for anyone who was willing to publish my articles (even if they didn't pay me), which included the newspaper for which I sold advertising space, the magazine I was later hired to run, and

< 157 >

assorted publications here and there. The desire to do the work was a given; in fact, *desire* is an understatement. The *ability* aspect was shaky in those early years and again when I started my own business. In both situations, I knew how much I *didn't* know, first, about writing and, later, about all the kinds of writing I would be called upon to do.

Each aspect of work presents its own challenges but none so much as having enough work to keep one financially afloat. Some people seem to be blessed in this area. Their companies downsize them out of their jobs but hire them back as consultants. Those core clients are sometimes enough to support a writer while he or she is building a business around them. Others specialize in specific industries or subject areas, such as sports, travel, agriculture, healthcare, training, science, or technology. They build strong reputations in those niches and attract assignments like magnets.

Many of us, however, have to struggle to land enough big projects or well-paying clients to sustain us. If you doubt it, just check out all of the websites devoted to helping writers find, promote, or sell their work. The list is long, but the advice is pretty much the same. The "secret" of landing assignments or clients or selling an article, a short story, or a book is an organized, ongoing marketing effort. The key words here are *organized* and *ongoing*. If that were easy we would all be doing it and drowning in work. But it isn't easy, for many reasons.

One is that, when we do have work, we devote every ounce of energy and moment of time to doing it. It is only when we make the deadline, send it out the door, and let out

< 158 >

a sigh of relief that we may notice an absence of other work to do. We've been so busy working that we didn't have time to fill the pipeline. The result is often sheer panic, followed by frantic phone calls to clients, prospects, editors, other writers, and sources. Obviously, we should have been marketing all along. But it is difficult to find the work, do the work, service clients, keep in contact with editors, send out bills, pay bills, and all the myriad tasks it takes to run a business. Add to that the fact that we may have a life of some kind, and it all seems next to impossible. When and how are we supposed to do it all?

The point is that we *must* do it, or we won't last very long in this business. Although everything may seem equally crucial, let's focus on only one aspect: finding work. What does an organized, ongoing marketing effort entail, and how can you fit it into your already overflowing schedule? Here are some suggestions:

- **Be proactive, not reactive.** Don't wait until the pipeline is empty to suddenly start getting your name out there. If you create some sort of a direct mail, follow-up marketing plan, it may take you weeks to land a job. By that time you'll feel and sound desperate, which will come across in your correspondence and conversations. The best time to "job hunt" is when you have a job and aren't in a panic to find one.

- **Think of marketing as one of your two top priorities**—the other being writing. If it's at the top of your list,

< 159 >

staring you in the face every day, you are more likely to do it. Decide how much time you need to do it right, and schedule that in your planner. At first, it may seem an interruption in your workflow, but eventually you'll find it to be both valuable and a necessary break from work, work, work.

- **Develop a system of organization.** It doesn't have to be elaborate; it just has to be used. There are many client management and scheduling programs available; in this age of computer technology, using white index cards and a calendar is like writing on parchment with a quill pen. If you learn and correctly utilize any of these programs, you will save time and never accidentally misplace a contact or forget to make an important phone call.

- **Keep your name and message in front of people—** with reminder cards, regular e-mails, brochures, a website, advertising, print or on-line newsletters, press releases, regular phone calls, networking, and face-to-face meetings. Overwhelming? Not if you carve out even an hour a day to market and do it in a purposeful way.

- **Try to enjoy yourself.** Going places, making contacts, talking to people, focusing on what others need instead of selling yourself can be rewarding and fun, if you use a light touch. Even if you don't consider yourself an extrovert, the more you do this, the more natural it will seem. That's when it ceases to be "work."

< 160 >

CHAPTER 36

MAKING DEADLINES

make (mâk) *verb*
made (mâd) **mak·ing, makes** *verb, transitive*
1. To cause to exist or happen; bring about; create:
made problems for him; making a commotion.
2. To bring into existence by shaping, modifying, or
putting together material; construct: *make a dress.*
3. To cause to be or become: made her position clear;
a decision that made him happy.

dead·line (dèd līn″) *noun*
1. A time limit, as for payment of a debt or completion
of an assignment.
2. A boundary line in a prison that prisoners can cross
only at the risk of being shot.

If there are two professions that live and die by deadlines
they are writing and graphic design. Journalists, in particular,
know that deadlines are sacrosanct; you *must* make them,
even if it means staying up all night to do it. Many of us speak
from experience when we recall how many times we have
done that over the years. What is really frustrating is when
you kill yourself to get a story to an editor who doesn't get to
it for a week or so or a project to a client who absolutely had

< 161 >

to have it on that day but isn't in the office that day or even that week. Those are the times you may ponder the unfairness of life, but such ponderings do not cause you to miss the next deadline, even if it's for the same person.

What is this mysterious hold deadlines have on writers? If every single freelance writer had once been a reporter, it would be easier to understand; but I, for one, never was a reporter. The closest I came to drop-dead deadlines was in the magazine business when the printer date was nonnegotiable. If we didn't get the boards (yes, this was before digital files) to the printer on time, our publication would be rescheduled, printed late, mailed late, and delivered late. Those were truly grounds for termination. I don't know your particular story; but I'm betting that, somewhere along the way, you have had a similar experience, which left an indelibly etched lesson.

Deadlines are serious business, especially for a freelancer. They attest to your dependability and professionalism. Often, they have financial implications, as in the above example with printers' schedules. They are rarely isolated events, i.e., each deadline may be a step in a series, leading up to the most important one. That is why magazines and annual reports are planned from the mail date, backwards, to the very first activity. Although there are instances when an editor or client will demand something by a given date, which turns out to be meaningless, they are few and far between. *Your* job is to make the deadline; what others do with the material once they receive it is not the point.

< 162 >

The first key to making deadlines is planning. Always ask when the project is due, and get a specific date. Knowing your destination enables you to map out the trip. Let's assume the project is a newsletter, and you are responsible for delivering copy only. The example I'll use is a high-impact, four-page, glossy newsletter for a multifaceted company. I have done many newsletters over the years, but this one proved to be the biggest challenge by far. The client was new, and I was unfamiliar with the company and its areas of specialization. The publication was to be the second issue of a newsletter that had been designed in-house and written by another freelancer. The first issue had taken many months to complete. This one, we hoped, would go more smoothly.

Here is the scenario—the way it *should* have gone and the way it actually unfolded:

- Meet with the client to determine direction, content, sources of information, and timetable. *(Step one went well, and I was able to guide the discussion and help map out the purpose and potential layout of articles.)*

- Follow up with a recap of meeting, plan for proceeding, estimated fee structure, and schedule of payments. *(This had to be approved by the president. The client was not willing to pay my estimated fee—a red flag. I agreed to do it for less, which turned out to be a mistake. Actual work done was twice the original estimate.)*

< 163 >

- Begin research and interviews. *(I read every existing piece of background and promotional literature; the editor set up the interview schedule, which included nineteen people.)*

- Interview, on tape. *(These took place in random order, subject to the availability of the interviewees. The schedule was intense and often included several people at one time or several interviews in one day.)*

- Transcribe interviews. *(This was incredibly time-consuming due to the number and complexity of the interviews.)*

- Write the articles, and turn in drafts to editor. *(These had to be reviewed by the editor and the sources of information, who were often difficult to pin down. The time lag between turning in the drafts and getting feedback was often weeks—another red flag.)*

- Correct or rewrite drafts as required. *(This was almost always required, sometimes more than once.)*

- Make final corrections; and secure approval by editor, sources, and president. *(At the time I originally wrote this chapters, none of those things had occurred. Not all sources had read, commented on, or approved copy. The president had not reviewed it. Final corrections were not been made—third red flag.)*

< 164 >

- Turn in final copy, and send final invoice. *(The project is on hold in deference to more pressing internal priorities; invoice has been submitted. From inception of the project to the present, a year has passed with no explanation.)*

The lesson here is this: Deadlines are a two-way street. As you are expected to make yours, clients have an obligation to meet theirs, for all of the same reasons mentioned in paragraph three.

< 165 >

CHAPTER 37

JUGGLING ASSIGNMENTS

jug·gle (jŭg´el) *verb*
jug·gled, jug·gling, jug·gles *verb, transitive*
1. To keep (two or more objects) in the air at one time by
alternately tossing and catching them.
2. To have difficulty holding a position; balance insecurely.
3. To keep (more than two activities, for example) in motion or progress at one time: *managed to juggle a full-time job and freelance writing.*

as·sign·ment (e-sìn´ment) *noun*
1. The act of assigning.
2. Something, such as a task, that is assigned.
See synonyms for task.

Once upon a time, there was a young feature writer who had mastered the art of concentration—on one article at a time. Stories B, C, and D would have to wait patiently in the wings until the star of the show, story A, had been thoroughly researched, absorbed, written, polished, and turned in to the editor. Only then could story B move to center stage. It was a tidy, organized approach to writing—giving my all to every

< 166 >

project, one project at a time—and, for many years, it worked flawlessly.

That was back when all I did was write. I had no other job responsibilities, which made it a perfect arrangement. My pattern was so ingrained and accepted by everyone that, when I was ready to write, I was permitted to do it at home. This was unheard of in the context of the magazine for which I worked. At first, my editor was aghast. "Haven't you ever worked for a newspaper?" he would bark. "Good reporters can write in the middle of a three-ring circus."

"No," I would reply. "I have never worked for a newspaper, and I can't write in the middle of a three-ring circus." Of course, writing in one room, while everything from gymnastic practice to giggling pajama parties were going on in the next, was a bit distracting, but I never mentioned that. So I wrote at home, came back to the office after a ten or twelve-hour marathon at the typewriter, turned in my masterpiece, and started over. I thought that was the way everybody worked.

My well-ordered, one-thing-at-a-time writing life came to an abrupt end when I moved into the corporate world, where it was a miracle to complete one page, let alone a whole story, without interruptions. Multiple stories, multiple publications, multiple tasks turned every day into a mishmash of unrelated activities. While I was interviewing for one article, I was writing another, running around taking photos, laying out a newsletter, working with a designer, sitting in a meeting, fielding phone calls, writing memos, or something—often several somethings at the same time.

< 167 >

It was an agonizing adjustment, which I never really mastered until I became a marketing manager. Then, it was either go crazy or learn to manage the chaos. I learned to manage it, which turned out to be my salvation in that job and later in my own business. I also learned that, if life is not neat and orderly, work is even less so. Here are some of the other hard-won lessons I acquired along the way:

- **Compartmentalize.** There are many ways to organize multiple assignments. One is to group related projects in one area of your desk, so that you can work on more than one at a time if the spirit moves you. A similar approach is to break large, complicated jobs into smaller, doable parts and attack one part at a time. Another is to arrange jobs in order of priority, from the ones with drop-dead deadlines down to those that allow more time or are less important. You might try positioning the jobs you like least at the top, so that you will do them first. Whatever system you use, just make sure that it makes sense to you and that you use it.

- **Conceptualize.** View each assignment holistically. What is its objective? If it's complex, what's the best way to break it up? Is there a logical order to what needs to be accomplished? What is your deadline? If you work backwards from there, how much time do you have for each part? When should you begin?

- **Concentrate.** Once you choose the particular project you are going to work on, lock onto it like a magnet. Give it

< 168 >

your total attention for the time you are doing it, then put it down and forget it. That kind of focus, where you are so thoroughly engrossed that time simply stops, has been described as "flow" by author Mihaly Csikszentmihalyi or likened to meditation by practitioners of Zen.

- **Complete.** When you pull away from what you're doing, whatever the reason, don't just abandon it and grab the next thing on your list. Bring each activity to closure, put it away, and do something totally unrelated to help you shift gears. Take a walk, do the dishes, run the vacuum, work out—whatever it takes to clear your mind. Then, you can bring a fresh perspective and renewed energy to the next task on your list.

- **Control the clutter.** There's an old saying about having to break eggs in order to make an omelet. Apparently, some of us have to make a mess in order to write. I'm always amazed at the litter I create in my office while I'm working. Somewhere between completing job #1 and moving on to job #2, take a few minutes to bring order to chaos. A tidy working environment is much more conducive to clear thinking than a messy one. Perhaps that's why so many writers seem to spend more time straightening up our offices than working.

< 169 >

CHAPTER 38

EVERYTHING COUNTS

eve·ry·thing (èv´rê-thîng˝) *pronoun*
1. a.) All things or all of a group of things. b.) All relevant matters: *told each other everything.*
2. The most important fact or consideration: *In business, timing is everything.*

count (kount) *verb*
count·ed, count·ing, counts *verb, transitive verb, intransitive*
1. To have importance.
2. To have a specified importance or value.
3. To matter; to be of significance.

Remember that great TV commercial where a young woman is negotiating a very important deal over the phone? The others on her conference call hear the voice of a sharp, confident professional. We, however, see her sitting at her computer, wearing pajamas and bunny slippers. The bunny slippers redefined casual attire for those of us who work at home. After all, if no one can see you, all you have to do is act the part, and no one will be the wiser.

The point of this chapter is that you must do more than *act* the part; you must *live* the part. As a freelance writer, you

< 170 >

are always "on," even when you're home alone, looking like something the cat dragged in. Unless you use Skype or GoToMeeting for every call, you can wear anything you want and look as awful as you can look ... right? So, what if you're still in a robe or sweats? What difference does it make? Just because others can't see you doesn't mean they can't hear your voice when you speak; and the voice, more than the words, speaks volumes. If you are dressed in a suit, you sound like you've got it altogether, naturally. When you're wearing a torn T-shirt and running shorts, you have to put some energy into how you come across.

I used to work in an office that didn't have a dress code. People wore pretty much what they wanted with the exception of jeans. But one sales rep always wore a pressed white shirt and tie. Why? Because he felt better and more in control of the sales call, which is the way he viewed his phone calls. His confidence was up, and that was obvious in his demeanor and his voice.

Think of life as a marketing call. Wherever you are (in a client's office, at the theater, or racing through the grocery store) and whatever you're doing (selling a story, attending a conference, or hosting a dinner party), you are projecting an indelible image to those around you. It is far better to project the image *you* want than to have it created for you by default.

Everything counts, from your clothes and grooming to your preparation and punctuality, and everything in-between. This may seem artificial or self-conscious to you, and, at first, it may be a little of both. But, whether you are aware of it or not, everything you say and do, every way in which you

< 171 >

present yourself to the world, and every mannerism or annoying habit you may have is creating an impression in the minds of others. Whether those impressions are accurate or completely skewed, to those people, they are true. To them, perception *is* reality.

"Everything counts" means just that. Pick up any book on image (*Polishing Your Professional Image* by yours truly is an oldie but goody), and you will read pretty much the same thing. The basic advice is be aware of how you are coming across to others, which is not always easy because we see what we want to see and fix those things we don't like. How do you know how you're coming across? Look in the mirror, listen to yourself in conversation, replay your voice mail message, look over your corporate identity materials; and, when all else fails, ask a few people you trust to tell you the truth.

Since there are many, many books on professional image, and this is not one of them, let me offer just a few things I've tried.

- **Become an observer of people.** I love to do this in airports and office buildings. Even a quick glance will create an instant, all-encompassing impression of someone's general appearance, attractiveness, posture, clothing, grooming, and self-confidence. In only a moment, you have taken another person's measure and either approved or dismissed him or her. If you don't believe it, give it a try. You'll be shocked at how quickly you form an opinion based on appearance only and how judgmental you are.

< 172 >

• **Turn the tables, and imagine that you are being observed in the same way.** What do others see and sense? Do you pass or fail the two-second scan? What would you think if you were outside yourself, observing you as you meet someone new, walk into a reception area, or work the room at a networking event?

• **Take a ruthless inventory of every aspect of your personal presentation.**

✓ Appearance (wardrobe, hair, eye wear, accessories and jewelry, grooming, style)

✓ Physical traits (your voice in person and on the phone; just listen to any interview you have conducted on tape or call your voice mail from another phone), physical or verbal mannerisms, idiosyncrasies (usually hard to identify by yourself)

✓ Psychological traits (Are you upbeat, negative, self-deprecating, controlling, a know-it-all, full of yourself?)

✓ Conversational style (Do you talk more than listen, interrupt, interrogate, pontificate, or find yourself at a loss for words?)

✓ Professionalism (everything from your stationery and business cards to how promptly you return phone calls or follow through on commitments)

Years ago, when I was researching one of my very first books—*Polish Your Professional Image*—I interviewed young professionals, business executives, image consultants, and psychologists. From those interviews emerged

< 173 >

the theme of that little book and my personal approach to professional image.

- Professional image must be based on *respect*: respect for yourself and respect for others.
- Self-respect grows out of *authenticity*—being real, genuine, and completely natural.
- Respect for others implies *appropriateness*—behaving in a way that is suitable for a particular person, occasion, or place.

In the best of all worlds, there is a perfect balance between authenticity and appropriateness and, thus project exactly what you would like others to perceive.

< 174 >

CHAPTER 39

WEARING ALL THE HATS

wear (wâr) *verb*
wore (wôr, wor) **worn** (wôrn, worn) **wear·ing, wears**
1. To carry or have on the person as covering, adornment, protection, or role
2. To carry or have habitually on the person, especially as an aid: *wears glasses.*
3. To bear, carry, or maintain in a particular manner.

hat (hàt) *noun*
A role or an office symbolized by or as if by the wearing of different head coverings: *wears two hats—one as parent and one as corporate executive.*

One of the biggest decisions I ever made was to start "my own business," which is how I defined a full-time freelance writing career. Calling it a business was my way of proving to the world, and to myself, that this was no lark; it was a serious commitment. The fact that I knew nothing about running a business did not deter me. Naiveté is both the salvation and downfall of every entrepreneur. Most of us might think twice about taking the plunge if we knew what we were getting into. On the other hand, *not* knowing is the reason many such enterprises never get off the ground or, if

< 175 >

they do, eventually crash back to earth. Ignorance is *not* bliss, and running a business is far more complicated than I, for one, ever dreamed it would be.

Of course, not everyone who reads this book is or even wants to be a full-time freelance writer. Readers may run the gamut from dreamers and dabblers to those whose entire sustenance depends on income from independent writing. But whatever time you spend at this, if you are earning money, you must consider freelancing as a business. In that little corner of your life, you wear all the hats, from CEO to cleanup crew.

Some time ago, I read a book called *The E Myth Revisited: Why Most Small Businesses Don't Work and What To Do About It*,[1] by Michael E. Gerber. The author presents the most incredibly simple yet startling analysis of why so many of us fail. "The problem," writes Gerber, "is that everybody who goes into business is actually three people in one: the entrepreneur, the manager, and the technician." Each of these people has a distinct role, explains Gerber. The entrepreneur is the dreamer, the visionary, the one who wants to grow the business. The manager is more practical. It is his or her job to run the business, pay the bills, buy the supplies, keep track of schedules, and send out invoices. The technician is what Gerber calls "the doer." This is the expert, the part of us with the talent and skills—the writer. Before I read

---

1. *The E-Myth Revisited: Why Most Small Businesses Don't Work and What to Do About It*, Michael E. Gerber, Harperbusiness, a division of Harpercollins Publishers 1955.

< 176 >

this book, I might have listed a dozen hats we have to wear; Michael Gerber gets it down to three—all equally essential to survival and success.

What an eye opener this was for me! If I wanted to support myself, I had to do more than just write. I had to run my business on a day-to-day basis and grow my business by marketing. In a burst of insight I realized that I had no desire to do all those little things a manager must do, nor did I seem to have the time to market. The only time it occurred to me was when I was out of projects. The rest of the time I was too busy meeting deadlines to think about filling the pipeline.

By the time I had this epiphany, I was already running a full-time business that went far beyond writing to encompass project management, photography, consulting, lecturing, writing books, and self-publishing. I was swamped and enjoying only one aspect of my split personality: "the technician."

All I had ever wanted to do was write, but I was drowning in minutia. But if I did write all the time, who would do everything else? This is a serious question. Managing and growing a business are full-time jobs in themselves. Unless you do them during the day and write all night, it's hard to imagine how a single individual can do the work of three. Add to that juggling act the fact that you may have another job, a full-time family, myriad responsibilities, and possibly a social life; and it seems impossible.

Let me say at the outset that I don't have a magic solution. If I did, I would probably be in much better financial shape

< 177 >

than I am. However, after twenty-five years (at this writing), I have learned a few things about keeping my balance. Let's start with two assumptions: Your strong suit is doing the work—writing—so you don't need help in that department. On the other hand, you do need help running and developing your business.

Managing a business is a left-brained activity. To do it you must be organized, persistent, thorough, and detail oriented. What you do in this role makes it possible for your other two selves to write, earn a living, and find more work. Some people genuinely revel in detail and creating order out of chaos. I am not one of them nor, I suspect, are too many creative people. Somehow, we seem to do better at creating chaos than bringing order to it. Running a business takes time, and time, as they say, is money.

I would rather do *anything* than administrative work, but unless I become triplets, this is one hat I can't ignore. If you don't want to do it yourself you will probably have to hire someone to do it for you. I know you think you can't afford to do that, but, in reality, you can't afford *not to do it.* I was fortunate; I hired my daughter, who somehow manages to hold down a full-time teaching job *and* act as my personal assistant. She began by paying the bills, then took on all of the financial responsibilities. She also transcribed my interview tapes, proofread my terrible typing, dealt with all those pesky details that take fifteen phone calls to unscramble, did research on the Internet, ran errands when necessary, and generally kept me sane. All good things must come to end,

< 178 >

and this perfect arrangement was no exception. Eventually, my assistant quit her part-time job.

The third hat is the one worn by the part of you that dreams big dreams or is practical enough to know that, if you don't market, you run the risk of starving to death. Developing your business can mean anything from finding occasional assignments and earning enough to meet your present goals to taking on more business than one person can handle, adding staff, and moving to larger quarters. Wherever you find yourself, one thing is certain: you *must* have a steady stream of work to do, and that work is not likely to fall in your lap. (OK, *sometimes* it does, but not all the time or forever.)

Frankly, if I could, I would hire a rep or someone to set up appointments for me. If my other daughter didn't live out of town, she would be my first choice. She can sell anything to anyone, so surely she could sell me. If delegating your marketing efforts is not in the cards, you will have to bite the bullet and write the letters, query the editors, make the calls, meet the clients, and personally secure the assignments. At best, it will result in new projects. At the very least, it will get you away from your computer and out of your office occasionally. The solitary life of a writer can be seductive and isolating. Marketing forces you to interact with other humans, which, in turn, feeds your creativity.

Marketing also takes time and energy; unfortunately, it is where most of us drop the ball. The only way to get it done is to do it, even if it's only an hour a day. I have a friend who

< 179 >

is out and about every single day. He spends as much time finding new business as he does working. And this man is always busy, always having fun, always making money. He is an inspiration to me.

If you really want to write every waking minute of your day, you have two ways of handling your other roles: play them yourself or find an understudy. The only choice you *don't* have is to ignore them.

< 180 >

CHAPTER 40

ADMINISTRATIVE STUFF

ad·min·is·tra·tion (àd-mĭn´ĭ-strâ´shen) *noun*
1. Management, especially of business affairs.
2. Management of an institution, public or private.
— ad·min´is·tra´tive (-strâ´tĭv, -stre-) *adjective*

stuff (stŭf) *noun*
1. The material out of which something is made or formed; substance.
2. The essential substance or elements; essence: *"We are such stuff as dreams are made on"* (Shakespeare).

In the preceding chapter, I referred to a book called *The E-Myth Revisited: Why Most Small Businesses Don't Work and What To Do About It* by Michael E. Gerber, in which the author describes the three personalities that live within each of us—the entrepreneur, the manager, and the technician. It is the manager who runs the business side of the business and thus is in charge of the *administrative stuff*. I believe I also mentioned that this is not my strong suit.

While it probably isn't your strong suit either, it is a reality; and unless you are independently wealthy, you must attend to it. So, this will be a nuts-and-bolts chapter on what the

< 181 >

manager in you must do to keep your business afloat while your other two personalities are finding and doing the work.

- **Schedule and keep track of appointments.** If you have ever failed to show up for an appointment, you know first-hand how embarrassed you felt and what impression you created in the mind of the person you were supposed to meet. If you rely on your memory or a scribbled note on a post-it to keep your appointments straight, chances are good this *will* happen to you, if it hasn't already. Your system can be as high tech as scheduling and calendar software or as unsophisticated as index cards and a generic planner.

  The point is you *must* have a system. When you make an appointment, record the person's name, phone number, date, time, and reason for the meeting in two places: your scheduling system *and* your daily planner. The trick is to check your planner one or two days ahead to see what appointments you have coming up. *Always* confirm the day before you are to meet. I can't tell you the number of times I have scheduled a meeting for a different day and time than my contact has scheduled it. It doesn't matter who was correct; what matters is that the meeting did not occur.

- **Keep your promises, and adhere to deadlines.** Trust is a delicate thing; it may take years to build, yet mere moments to smash it to pieces. It doesn't take very long for a person to figure out that, when you say you'll do

< 182 >

something, chances are good you won't. How many times has someone said to you, "I'll get back to you on that," or "I'll put that in the mail right away," or "I'll pass your name along to so-and-so," and forgotten the promise as soon as it was uttered? Is a simple remark like, "I'll call you" really a promise? In my mind, it is.

Perhaps it's the way I was raised. When my parents said, "We'll go to the movies on Sunday," unless someone had 103° fever, we went to the movies on Sunday. Conversely, if I said, "I'll clean up my room this afternoon," I was expected to do just that, *before* dinner. An offhand remark may seem to be a small thing, but small things add up to trust or lack of it. If you say you will do something, do it. If you don't intend to or can't do it, don't say you will.

- **Market for new business, and network.** This is really your entrepreneur's job, but that part of you is notorious for dreaming big dreams and letting it go at that. *You're* the one who has to push, prod, and turn those dreams into reality. It will be up to *you* to write the letters, proof them for errors, get them mailed, and schedule the follow-up calls and face-to-face meetings. Networking is another matter. While the entrepreneur shows up to schmooze with the crowd, it will be *your* job to determine which crowd is worth the time and trouble. Some places and events are well worth the time; others are a colossal waste. Someone has to decide which is which and take care of getting the right ones on the calendar.

< 183 >

- **Manage your database of clients and/or editors.** Your database is gold, especially if it is well researched and up to date. It is your lifeline to new business or to ongoing business with current clients or editors. Every name on it should be there for a reason. It is a current, inactive, or potential client; a new lead, a media contact, or a referral source; an editor or a publisher. If the name has no real purpose, delete it. This is about quality, not quantity.

  Every name you do keep should have updated information on address, phone and fax numbers, e-mail address, website, secretary or assistant, brief history of interactions and transactions to date, last contact, last action taken, next action planned, and any information that will help you create and maintain a relationship with this person. You can do this on index cards, of course, but a client-management program can do amazing things *if* you take the time to learn how to use it properly. A database is useless if it isn't used, and you can't use it if it's an out-of-date mess.

- **Nurture your relationships.** As important as that database is, it merely *represents* people; it is not the people themselves. Freelance writing is a service business, and service means more than merely making deadlines and sending holiday cards. Service means developing and sustaining relationships, getting inside of a person to find out his or her real needs, and then going beyond the expected. It means knocking their socks off with consistent, above-and-beyond attention to everything you do.

< 184 >

- **Assign priorities to projects and tasks, and then do them in order of importance.** There isn't a time-management scheme out there that doesn't propose some method of separating tasks into groups. One program suggests four categories based on urgency and importance. Another assigns As, Bs, or Cs to every item, with As being the most critical and Cs often not even appearing on the radar screen. One advises dividing your calendar into blocks of time with each block representing a group of related tasks. Most systems counsel that time management begins with knowing your life's mission and working from there. Effective time management is a more complex process than making lists.

  Pick a system, or design your own way of assigning priorities. What matters is that you do the important things first, when you are fresh, and that you are disciplined enough to complete one thing at a time. Nothing feels better than checking off an item or drawing a line through it. It's tangible evidence that you have done something you said you would do.

- **Open mail, read and respond to e-mails, return phone calls, and go through your in-box.** The proverbial in-box is everybody's nightmare; but when you work at home, it can be as large as your office, dining-room table, or available floor space. Piles here, there, and everywhere are hardly conducive to an orderly mind. Clutter is a recipe for professional disaster. "I know what's in every one of those piles," people say, but I don't believe it. A good part

< 185 >

of the mess is probably unopened mail (could there be bills in there?), catalogues or magazines you never asked for and won't read, offers for 7 percent interest on a new credit card, this week's grocery store specials, and assorted junk mail. Calls to return are written down somewhere; but, even if you could find your notes, there really is no time set aside to do that. And the newest scourge, email, could take you all day, if you actually read and replied to every one you receive.

The solution? It's far too vast for one paragraph, but the short version is **get organized**. Enroll in a seminar or read a book. How about *Get Organized* by yours truly (Amacom, New York); *Organizing From the Inside Out*, by Julie Morgenstern (Owl Books, Henry Holt and Company, New York); or *First Things First* by Stephen R. Covey, A. Roger Merrill, and Rebecca R. Merrill (Simon and Schuster, New York)? And there are many, many more such titles at your local bookstore or library, Amazon, or your eBook reader.

- **Do errands, go to the post office, and buy office and computer supplies.** These activities can be seen as annoying interruptions because you have better things to do or as respites because they get you out of your office. No matter how you view them, they must be done, either by you or by someone you pay or coerce into doing them. They take time, they are not fun, and they make you feel unproductive. Like everything else your internal manager does, such activities must be scheduled and organized for efficient use of your time. Prime time is not the best slot for

< 186 >

them in your planner, but off-peak hours, evenings, or weekends would be just fine. If you worked in an office (remember when you did?), you did not run out and do your errands during the workday; but, somehow, you did get them accomplished, eventually. When time is money, and you are the only person working in your business, just apply those same constraints. Work during work time; get out and about after hours.

< 187 >

CHAPTER 41

MANAGING THE MONEY

man·age (màn´ĭj) *verb*
man·aged, man·ag·ing, man·ag·es *verb, transitive*
1. To direct or control the use of; handle: *manage a complex machine tool.*
2. To exert control over: *"Managing the news . . . is the oldest game in town"* (James Reston). *"A major crisis to be managed loomed on horizon"* (Time).
3. To direct the affairs or interests of: manage a company; an agency that manages performers. See synonyms for conduct.

mon·ey (mùn´ê) *noun*
plural **mon·eys** or **mon·ies**
1. A commodity, such as gold, or an officially issued coin or paper note that is legally established as an exchangeable equivalent of all other commodities, such as goods and services, and is used as a measure of their comparative values on the market.
2. The official currency, coins, and negotiable paper notes issued by a government.
3. Assets and property considered in terms of monetary value; wealth.

< 188 >

Money may not be the root of all evil, but it certainly is a source of stress in my life. I wish I could work for clients because I love them or their projects. I wish I never had to provide an estimate, send an invoice, or follow up on late (or no) payments. I wish we lived in a barter culture in which I could trade words for products and services. But, then, I would also like to see what it's like "somewhere over the rainbow," and that is not going to happen either. The fact is, most of us work to earn a living. We sell our time, talent, energy, and skills in the marketplace, and we expect to be paid for those things.

That's a fact of life or at least of business life. Supposedly, we know how much time we have invested in a project, what our efforts are worth, and how to carry on such a transaction in a civilized, professional manner. It should be a pragmatic activity, not an emotional one. After all, as we all remember that line from The Godfather, "It isn't personal; it's business." Perhaps, but to a creative person, all work is personal; and by extension, so is being fairly compensated.

Maybe it's that finances are a left-brained activity and creativity is a right-brained one. And maybe there are some writers and artists who handle monetary issues with as much confidence as they handle the tools of their trade. For the rest of us, however, the financial side of running our businesses can turn into a full-fledged phobia if we don't master the basics and get our hearts out of the equation. Here are the basics:

< 189 >

- **Hire an accountant,** preferably one who specializes in small businesses and will be accessible when needed. Work with that person to set up your business, even if it is just part-time freelancing. Ask him or her to answer the questions you don't know enough to ask and to give you a road map for what to do and how to do it.

- **Open a separate checking account for your business.** This will eliminate the confusion of trying to sort out what is a business expense and what is not. It also will clearly spell out what is coming in and what is going out—the point being that supposedly you can't spend money you don't have.

- **Use one credit card for business purposes,** and don't use it for anything else. If you get one that sends you an end-of-the-year itemized report of charges, that will simplify your record keeping enormously.

- **Invest in a time-and-billing software program.** I use iBiz, but I'm sure there are several other good ones out there. Such software does amazing things and often interacts with check-writing programs so that everything becomes part of a seamless process. It will keep perfect track of your time with a simple on/off switch and multiply that by your hourly rate. It will maintain a record of every client's or publication's information, agreements, projects,

< 190 >

invoices, and payments. It will create reports in as much or as little detail as you desire. And it will serve as proof that you put in the time you said you did.

- **Get it in writing.** Don't start anything without a signed letter of agreement stipulating what, when, and how much. Then, be prepared to live with your estimate or arrangement. This sounds easy, but you have to be extremely disciplined and self-confident to tell a client or editor that you won't begin the project until you have the signed contract in hand.

- **Send out invoices** at the same time every month, upon completion of a project, or at intervals—whatever has been agreed to on the front end. A time-and-billing program will set up a template for your bills and allow you to customize any aspect, from marking up expenses, to listing every activity and expense, to including personalized messages. These are just the basic things such software can do for you. Read the manual, or take a course to learn the finer points.

- **Follow up on late payments.** Spell out your terms at the outset and on your invoices. Send second and third notices. Then, make the phone call or perhaps more than one. If you say, "My lawyer will be in touch," be sure your lawyer writes a letter on firm letterhead. (It won't do any good unless you are planning to bring suit, but it looks impressive.) If you threaten to turn the matter over to a collection

< 191 >

agency, do it. If you say you will take the case to Small Claims Court, do it. A word of caution though: Small Claims Court is great in principle, not so great in practice.

Many things can go wrong, and I have experienced all of them. The defendant could not be found, so the notice has not been served. (You don't know that until your case is called). The defendant *has* been served but doesn't show. You win the case, but the defendant doesn't pay. You jump through all the right hoops to get your money; but the defendant closes the bank account, goes out of business, claims bankruptcy, or just disappears. The court has no jurisdiction to force payment; and it often costs you more in time, money (to have the papers served or the money collected), and aggravation than it's worth. Sound far-fetched? It isn't.

Here are some ways to manage your money and protect yourself:

• **Keep orderly records.** Keep track of *everything*, especially your expenses. Ask for, record, and file receipts. Know what is deductible and what is not. A good accountant will find legitimate deductions you never dreamed of. *Immediately* record mileage, parking charges, tips, reimbursable and billable expenses. If you don't do it on the spot, you will not remember. Believe me, it will go up in a puff of smoke.

< 192 >

- Save for taxes. That means putting away the correct percentage of *every fee* in a separate account. If you've never paid quarterly estimated taxes before, the first time they are due and you are caught unprepared will be the rudest of awakenings. It's a mistake you are not likely to make twice.

- Keep your own credit record clean. That means paying your own bills on time, not spending more than you can afford, and making wise purchasing decisions. While your clients may get away with not paying, you never will. Don't ask me why.

Sound like a lot of work? Well, that's because it is. On the other hand, when you set up the systems at the very beginning, with the help of your accountant and computer guru, managing your business finances will become as routine as brushing your teeth and as painless as such an activity can be for a right-brained writer.

< 193 >

CHAPTER 42

BURNOUT

burned-out (bûrnd´out´) or burnt-out
(bûrnt´out´) *adjective*
Worn out or exhausted, especially as a result of
long-term stress.

The word *burnout* was not even in my vocabulary when I first started writing. I knew that I would *never* tire of it, *never* want to do anything else, *never* stop. I wrote at every opportunity; and most of those were after work, after the dinner dishes were done, after the dog had been walked, and after the kids were finally in bed. Looking back, I don't know how I did it, except that I was young and obsessed. I ran on adrenaline and addiction to writing, I suppose. All I wanted in life was to write full time.

"You won't love it so much when your avocation turns into a vocation," friends warned me. "*Now*, it's exciting; then, it will be just a job." It is now forty-five years later, and I'm still at it. To be honest, I have swallowed more than one of those "nevers" during my career. Let me clarify up front that I am a writer to my very core. There is nothing in the world I would rather do; and, when I toy with the idea of my next career, no matter what it may be, it will involve writing. I

< 194 >

may not devote myself to writing books or to teaching, but I'll probably die at my computer.

Having said that, I must admit that I have been worn out, exhausted, and blocked more than a few times over the years. Being a full-time writer means you write *all the time*. That's pretty much all you do, except for gathering the information you will write about. My first full-time job was as the editor of a city magazine. It didn't take me long to discover that my predecessor had left me nothing. I mean *nothing*: no plans, no manuscripts, no names of writers or suppliers, no P&L statements. It was overwhelming, not only because I would have to write everything, but because I didn't know the first thing about running a magazine.

That was my first experience with on-the-job training and major burnout. After little more than a year into the job I found myself in a hospital with pneumonia. I lived (though that was touch and go for a while) and left. I swore that I would never marry a job again. Yeah, right. My second job released me from managing an entire magazine, but I was still writing most of it. I spent six years researching, interviewing, and writing hundreds of feature articles. I'd finish one and immediately plunge into the next, which was always just a bit more complicated or challenging than the one before it. By the end of that job, I was practically brain dead and still broke (the money thing is another whole story).

The rest of my resume is a variation on that theme. From magazines, I went into corporate communications, where I did exactly the same things: researched, interviewed, and

< 195 >

wrote—this time, multiple publications—for another four years. Along the way, I added photography and layout to my collection of skills. In my last position, I moved into marketing communications and management, along with writing, and kept on keeping on for another six-and-a-half years. If I was burned out at that point, it was more with the vicissitudes of corporate life than with writing; but, to be sure, I *was* burned out.

For the past twenty-five years, I have been a business owner, a one-woman band, and a full-time writer. When frustration has reared its head, it has been caused by the need to create some sort of balance among doing the work, finding the work, serving clients, and attending to the unbelievable number of administrative and financial tasks that come with the job.

The writing has been the most varied I have ever done, comprising virtually every industry, every subject, and every genre. The variety has stretched me, educated me, and improved my work. What has driven me crazy is the uncertainty of finding work when there is too little, doing the work when there is too much, holding on to the work in the midst of a chaotic business environment, and continuing to love the work no matter what it entails. Keeping all of those balls in the air all the time sometimes seems impossible.

One last fact: During all of this time, I have freelanced. In the beginning, I did it while I worked at an unrelated job; in the middle, I did it in addition to being an employed writer; and, for the past twenty-five years, I have done it full time. In

< 196 >

a sense, I am still writing on the side, since the books have been written "on my own time," so to speak. "Prime time" is reserved for earning a more dependable living.

Here is what I have learned that may be of help to you when you see BURNOUT in neon on your computer screen.

• **Never say never.** This advice applies to everything in life. It is the one word that is guaranteed to trip you up because we never (whoops) know what life is going to throw at us or how we will feel when we must deal with the unexpected.

• **Admit it.** You're tired. You're sick of what you're doing. You hate your editor/client. You're uninspired. You have writer's block. You wish you were a carpenter. You want to scream. The point is, don't deny it and fight your way through it. Stop, and be aware of what's going on inside of you. The body never lies, and, if it's turning into pretzel knots, there is a reason.

• **Don't panic.** When you feel yourself burning out, getting tired, writing mechanically, or feeling too blocked to write at all—and you will—take a break. (Oh, but I can't; I have a deadline!) Yes, I know, but whatever you're doing or not doing isn't working. So, stop and take a walk, a nap, or a vacation; or go to a movie. Read a book, veg out in front of the TV, put on your favorite CD, wash the floor, fix your car, do yoga or tai chi or karate. Do anything but write.

< 197 >

- **Know that it will pass.** You are still a writer, a good writer in fact. You haven't lost your skill or your love of the craft. It's probably premature to throw up you hands in defeat and job hunt. Be a Taoist: Go with the flow. You don't beat yourself to death when you have the flu; why do it when you are suffering from temporary malaise? Chalk it up to a passing phase, and get on with your life.

- **Think it through.** If it's serious, if it's continuous, if it's painful, and it won't go away, you may have to do more than go to a movie or roller blading. You may have to examine what is going on and whether it is indeed time to move on to something else. My guess is, that given time, you'll find some way to refresh your mind and your creativity. But if that doesn't happen, you have a right to switch gears and find another outlet for your talents. You did not sign a life-long contract to be a freelance writer. If it's time to do something else, go for it.

< 198 >

CHAPTER 43

WORK AND FAMILY

work (wûrk) *noun*
1. Physical or mental effort or activity directed toward the production or accomplishment of something.
2. a.) A job; employment. b.) A trade, profession, or other means of livelihood.
3. a.) Something that one is doing, making, or performing, especially as an occupation or undertaking; a duty or task. b.) An amount of such activity either done or required.
4. a.) The part of a day devoted to an occupation or undertaking: met her after work. b.) One's place of employment.

fam·i·ly (fàm′e-lê, fàm′lê) *noun*
plural **fam·i·lies**
1. a.) A fundamental social group in society typically consisting of a man and woman and their offspring.
   b.) Two or more people who share goals and values, have long-term commitments to one another, and reside usually in the same dwelling place.
2. All the members of a household under one roof.

< 199 >

I must begin this chapter with a disclaimer: At this time in my life, I do not have to juggle my business and a live-at-home family. I am no longer married, and my daughters have their own homes. So, what I have to say about this particular balancing act obviously does not reflect my current situation. Nonetheless, for many, many years, my life revolved around work and family, each of which demanded 100 percent of my effort and energy. The memories are vivid.

The family came first; the writing didn't make its appearance until almost a decade later. I had a husband and two very active young children. Writing, which began as a lark, turned into an adventure and ultimately became a consuming passion. In the meantime, I was a wife and a mother with all the myriad responsibilities that role demanded. It was still the era of "Father Knows Best" and "The Donna Reed Show," which meant shirt-waist dresses, dinner on the table every night at six, and driving a station wagon full of little people to and from nursery school. I wrote in stolen moments, when the girls were in school or after they went to bed.

In the beginning, writing had to be squeezed in between all of the other stuff of life. I'm sure it was viewed as a "hobby" by my family, but all of that changed when I landed my first job as a full-time writer. That's when the competition between the two halves of my life really intensified. By that time, I was a single parent, in addition to being a floundering new editor of a city magazine. My little girls were probably the original latchkey kids. They could let themselves in the house and make peanut butter and jelly sandwiches, but that didn't stop them from calling me one hundred times a day.

< 200 >

There never seemed to be enough of me to go around. The hours at work were long and stressful; my salary was a joke; and my health zigzagged all over the place.

Each step in my career brought more responsibility, less flexibility, and longer commutes. Guilt became my constant companion. I was never a Brownie leader or a room mother. I didn't go on field trips or take an active role in the PTA. I remember being twenty miles away, interviewing a college president, when my editor called to tell me my youngest daughter had broken her arm, falling off the top of the cheerleaders' pyramid. The president was very gracious when I left suddenly.

On the bright side, I allowed gymnastics meets and disco practice in my living room; encouraged having friends sleep over; and subtly forced my daughters to learn to cook, the alternative being starving to death. I took some great pictures at real gymnastic meets and of the cheerleaders at football games, helped with many English papers, and learned to "edit on my eyelids" when the girls were in college. I tell you this because I now know this is how many writers live— employed, moonlighting, full-time, part-time, male, or female. In today's world, juggling roles is simply the way it is.

It was and is useless to haul around a bag of guilt and, obviously, beyond stressful to think you can do everything, be everywhere, and keep all those plates in the air without dropping one now and then. If I had it to do over again, I would do things differently.

< 201 >

- **I would face reality and kick the guilt.** "You gotta do what you gotta do," as they say; and feeling that you are failing your family doesn't help you, them, or your work.

- **I would communicate more assertively and less defensively.** If your family (husband, children, parents, whoever) understands the challenges you face, and you understand theirs, you can work together to help each other over the rough spots.

- **I would make and enforce a simple agreement.** When I'm working, please don't disturb me unless it is a *real* emergency; when we are together as a family, I won't let work interfere.

- **I would strive for balance in my life.** I would figure out what is truly important and what is extraneous. If you have your priorities straight, even if there are only two or three of them (work, family, yourself, not necessarily in that order), you won't constantly pour your energy down the drain.

- **I would put self-care high on that list of what is important.** If you run yourself into the ground, stress out, or get sick, you will be of little good as a writer, mother or father, spouse, or caretaker of an aging parent.

< 202 >

- **I would ease up on the perfectionism.** If you can't do it all, you certainly can't begin to do it all perfectly. When you die, do you really want your epitaph to read "She died with a bottle of Windex in her hand"?

< 203 >

CHAPTER 44

GETTING A LIFE

work (wûrk) *noun*
1. Physical or mental effort or activity directed toward the production or accomplishment of something.
2. a.) A job; employment. b.) A trade, profession, or other means of livelihood.
3. a.) Something that one is doing, making, or performing, especially as an occupation or undertaking; a duty or task: *begin the day's work.* b.) An amount of such activity either done or required: *a week's work.*
4. The part of a day devoted to an occupation or undertaking.

you (yo͞o) *pronoun*
1. Used to refer to the one or ones being addressed: *I'll lend you the book. You shouldn't work so hard. Did she telephone you from San Francisco?*
2. Used to refer to an indefinitely specified person; one: *You can't win them all.*

< 204 >

There are two approaches to work: one is working to live; the other is living to work. The difference defines a person's life, especially when that person is a freelance writer. Writing, for many of us, is a love affair, a calling. We didn't choose to do it; it chose us. Perhaps that sounds overly dramatic, but it is honestly the way I perceive my work. I am one of those who live to work. If I did not *have to* do it, I would do it anyway, as long as my work was writing.

I have friends who take the opposite position and cannot relate to my obsession. "Working *supports* a lifestyle; it is *not* a lifestyle," they insist. "You can love what you do and work hard at it, but its purpose is to let you enjoy the rest of your life." To such people, working is a means to an end. To me, it is an end in itself. There is no right or wrong here; there are only different perspectives. For many years, I was comfortable with mine. Writing was the center of my universe. Everything else simply revolved around it, like planets. It worked for me, so why change it?

Recently, as I have been working on this book, I have done quite a bit of thinking about this subject. Frankly, I am less certain that having my entire identity and all of my energy tied to a single aspect of my life, at the expense of all the others, is either wise or healthy. If a healthy life is a balanced life, mine is seriously out of kilter. Looking back, I realize that I have always been this way, with every job I've ever held and, certainly, since I have owned my own business. It never occurred to me that I was not having a life; to me, writing *was* my life.

< 205 >

But it occurs to me now. Work—writing—is more than a love affair; it is an addiction. Since I am writing to an audience of writers, your response might well be, "So, what's wrong with that?" Think of it this way: If I said, "My name is Bobbi, and I'm a workaholic," would it sound quite as enthralling? I think not. Any word that ends in "... *aholic*" should make one sit up and take notice.

Let me respond to the "What's wrong with that?" question. When one's life is seriously out of balance, everything suffers, including the thing that is getting most of the attention and energy. If your social life were the dominant theme, isn't it possible that your health, family, work, and intellectual sides might be getting short-changed? If you focused on your children to the exclusion of everything else, what would happen to your job, your intellectual or spiritual pursuits, and your creativity? You get the idea.

The old cliché, "All work and no play makes Jack a dull boy," didn't become a cliché for no reason. (I know that is politically incorrect, but it can't be helped.) Writers cannot afford to become dull. Creativity must be fed. Sitting alone in your office, fingers to keyboard, eyes fixed on your computer screen, is simply not enough. If that is all you do, you run a real risk of getting stale or burning out, both of which spell creative and professional death.

I am not advocating distancing yourself from your passion or your work. But I am suggesting that the more attention you pay to *all* of the parts of your life, the fresher and richer your writing will be. That is true whether you are working on

< 206 >

an article, a direct mail piece, or a book. Your mind is like a computer: nothing new in, nothing new out.

If you draw a wheel and put yourself at the hub, each of the spokes represents an important phase of a full and balanced life: creative, intellectual, emotional, social, spiritual, and physical. They all matter; they all contribute to each other; they are interdependent. What I have learned is this: If I attend to each of them, my writing is better, my work life is more satisfying, and my mind is more alert. My advice to writers, after all these years of not taking it myself, is this: Get a life. You'll be a better writer for it.

< 207 >

CHAPTER 45

PERSONAL BALANCE

per·son·al (pûr´se-nel) *adjective*

1. Of or relating to a particular person; private: *"Like their personal lives, women's history is fragmented, interrupted."* (Elizabeth Janeway).
2. a.) Done, made, or performed in person: a personal appearance. b.) Done to or for or directed toward a particular person: *a personal favor.*
3. Concerning a particular person and his or her private business, interests, or activities; intimate: *I have something personal to tell you.*

bal·ance (bàl´ens) *noun*

1. A stable mental or psychological state; emotional stability.
2. A state of equilibrium or parity characterized by cancellation of all forces by equal opposing forces.
2. A state of bodily equilibrium.
3. A harmonious or satisfying arrangement or proportion of parts or elements.

< 208 >

Is there really enough to say about balance to warrant one-third of a book? I have been asked more than once. The answer is *yes*. As a freelance writer, negotiating the delicate balance between your work life and your other life, the "other" often plays second fiddle to making a living. The question is, how can you effectively create and grow your business, maintain the freshness and quality of your writing, spend time with your family and friends, and occasionally even read a book? Part of the answer is to *give yourself a break*. Stop trying to be the perfect partner to your significant other or spouse; a model parent to your children; a caring son or daughter to your parents; the involved, loyal buddy to everyone you know; a fixture at the gym; and a regular attendee at your church, temple, mosque, fellowship, or meditation group? It is a set-up for failure to think any single individual could maintain a life designed for triplets.

If you aspire to be a working writer *and* have a full life on the other side of your office door, you can do both if you develop a strong, solid foundation. Stephen Covey, who became one of the country's most sought-after consultants after the publication of *The 7 Habits of Highly Effective People*[2], addressed this principle in his seventh habit: "Sharpen the Saw." I call it *personal balance*, but I think the underlying principles are much the same.

---

2. Stephen R. Covey, *The 7 Habits of Highly Successful People: Powerful Lessons in Personal Change* (New York , Simon & Schuster, 1989)

< 209 >

Personal balance is all about you. It's a gift you give yourself because you deserve it and because, without it, everything I've talked about in this book would be very difficult to attain and even harder to keep up. Personal balance is fundamental to becoming a healthy, well-rounded human being, whether you are a freelance writer, the CEO of a large corporation, or a professional golfer.

What *is* personal balance? What does it feel like? How do you create it, and how do you know when you have it? Let me begin with a disclaimer: I am neither a sage nor a philosopher. I *don't* know what it is and suspect I am not alone in not knowing. Yet, there have been moments in my life when I have experienced it. Personal balance is not enlightenment or Nirvana. Rather, it is a sense that all is right with the world and your place in it. Now, the question is, how do you make that happen?

If you visit the self-help section of any bookstore, you will find hundreds of books on how to find personal balance, though the titles may not use those exact words. Whatever they call it, authors have found that there's money to be made in how-to books on this subject. Considering how many I have read, I would certainly agree. Here is my distillation of what other authors advise.

Take time, make time for yourself. You're worth it, you deserve it, and you need it. Anne Morrow Lindbergh said it fifty years ago in her classic *Gift From the Sea*[3]. Cheryl

---

3. Anne Morrow Lindbergh, *Gift from the Sea* (New York, Pantheon Books, Inc., 1955)

< 210 >

Richardson said it more recently in *Make Time For Your Life*[4], one of Oprah's must-reads.

Forget for a moment that you have no time. It doesn't have to be huge blocks of time. Maybe it's just a couple of hours on a weekend or one whole evening that you proclaim as sacrosanct. The best advice I've read is, make a date with yourself, and keep it.

Set aside a little bit of that time to consider four critical aspects of your life: your physical and mental health, the state of your emotions, your relationships with others, and your spiritual practice, whatever it may be. How are you doing in those areas? Are you happy or stressed out of your mind? Are you feeling vibrantly energetic or more like a pile of wet laundry? Other than what you write about, is your mind atrophying from lack of stimulation? Do you meditate, pray, contemplate the mystery of life; or is all of that on the back burner because you can't fit it in.

While this is not an easy exercise or one you can complete in a short amount of time, it is worth exploring. One way to answer these questions is to catch yourself in the act of feeling hassled, coming down with a cold, telling your kids you're too tired to play, or vegging out in front of the TV instead of curling up with a book. Those are all clues to how you're really doing in these areas of your life.

---

4. Cheryl Richardson, *Make Time For Your Life: A Personal Coach's Seven-Step Program for Creating the Life You Want* (New York, Broadway Books, 1998)

< 211 >

Don't go off the deep end when you realize that your life is seriously skewed, and *you* are the one getting the short end of the stick. You probably knew that anyway. Instead, pick one thing to focus on. It could be as small as realizing that your daily nourishment consists of glazed donuts and whatever you happen to grab when you go in the kitchen, and that you are eating most meals at the computer. What if you had cereal or a protein milkshake for breakfast and a sandwich or a salad for lunch? And what if you took ten minutes anywhere but in your office to eat it? The answer is that you would have taken one step closer to achieving personal balance. You will be amazed at the power of these tiny changes.

< 212 >